# SCOTLAND
## from the Air

# SCOTLAND from the Air

## SECOND EDITION

by

Ann Glen

and

Michael Williams

'Auld Reekie'
a view of Edinburgh before recent 'clean
air' policies had come into operation.

Heinemann Educational Books
London

Heinemann Educational Books Ltd
LONDON EDINBURGH MELBOURNE AUCKLAND TORONTO
HONG KONG SINGAPORE KUALA LUMPUR
IBADAN NAIROBI JOHANNESBURG
LUSAKA NEW DELHI

ISBN 0 435 34363 7

Published by Heinemann Educational Books Ltd
48 Charles Street, London WIX 8AH
Printed in Great Britain by
Fletcher & Son Ltd, Norwich

# CONTENTS

| | | | |
|---|---|---|---|
| 1 | Introduction | Arable Farming; | 58 |
| 4 | Suilven; Sutherland | St. Abbs; Berwickshire | 60 |
| 6 | The Moor of Rannoch; Argyllshire | Westfield; Fife | 62 |
| 8 | The Great Glen; Inverness-shire | Bilston Glen; Midlothian | 64 |
| 10 | Ben Nevis; Inverness-shire | Longannet; Fife | 66 |
| 12 | Loch Lomond; Dunbartonshire and Stirlingshire | Loch Long; Argyllshire | 68 |
| 14 | The Eildon Hills; Roxburghshire | Grangemouth; Stirlingshire | 70 |
| 16 | The Cairngorm Mountains | Cruachan; Argyllshire | 72 |
| 18 | Plockton, Loch Carron; Wester Ross | Hunterston; Ayrshire | 74 |
| 20 | Loch Tay; Perthshire | The Big Mill; Ravenscraig, Motherwell, Lanarkshire | 76 |
| 22 | The Storr; Isle of Skye | Bathgate; West Lothian | 78 |
| 24 | Glencoe; Argyllshire | Newhouse Industrial Estate; Lanarkshire | 80 |
| 26 | The Grey Mare's Tail; Dumfriesshire | Selkirk; Selkirkshire | 82 |
| 28 | The River Spey; Morayshire | Lagavulin; an Islay Distillery, Argyllshire | 84 |
| 30 | The Isle of Arran; Buteshire | The Pulp Mill; Corpach, Inverness-shire | 86 |
| 32 | Glen Dochart; Perthshire | Invergordon; Ross and Cromarty | 88 |
| 34 | Ailsa Craig; Ayrshire | Communications; Dunbartonshire | 90 |
| 35 | The Bass Rock; East Lothian | The Hamilton By-Pass; Lanarkshire | 92 |
| 36 | Isle of Jura; Argyllshire | Kylesku; Sutherland | 94 |
| 38 | Balranald; North Uist, Inverness-shire | The Forth Bridges; Fife and West Lothian | 96 |
| 40 | Findhorn Bay; Morayshire | Prestwick; Ayrshire | 98 |
| 42 | Chanonry Point; Ross and Cromarty | The Crinan Canal; Argyllshire | 100 |
| 44 | Staffa; Inner Hebrides | Aberdeen; The Silver City | 102 |
| 46 | Forestry; Minard Forest, Argyllshire | Dundee; Angus | 104 |
| 48 | Inverpolly Forest; Ross and Cromarty | Edinburgh; The Old Town | 106 |
| 50 | Crofting; Lewis, Ross and Cromarty | Edinburgh; The New Town | 108 |
| 52 | Loch Katrine; Perthshire | Glasgow Docks | 110 |
| 54 | Hill-Farming; Glen Devon, Perthshire | Glasgow's Housing Problem | 112 |
| 56 | Dairy Farming; Dunbartonshire | Ayr; Ayrshire | 114 |

116    Linwood; Renfrewshire                     Kirkwall; Orkney                              138
118    Largs; Ayrshire                           Lerwick; Shetland                            140
120    Cumbernauld; Dunbartonshire               Gleneagles; Perthshire                       142
122    Glenrothes; Fife                          Muirfield; East Lothian                      144
124    Culross; Fife                             The Aviemore Centre; Inverness-shire         146
126    Perth; The Fair City                      Glen Shee; Perthshire                        148
128    Stirling; Stirlingshire                   The Cuillins; Isle of Skye                   150
130    Inveraray; Argyllshire                    Kippford; Kirkcudbright                       152
132    Oban; Argyllshire                         Nairn; County of Nairn                       153
134    Grantown-on-Spey; Morayshire              John O'Groats; Caithness                     154
136    Inverness; Inverness-shire

## Note on Local Authority Names

In May 1975, it is planned to replace all existing Local Authorities by 9 new Regions and 53 Districts. There will also be 3 new Island Authorities. As these changes had not taken place before this book went to press, the existing Authorities are used. There is a map showing the new Authorities inside the back cover.

# ACKNOWLEDGEMENTS

The authors and publishers would like to thank the following for permission to reproduce photographs on the pages indicated:

*The Scotsman*, 128; *Glasgow Herald and Evening Times*, 113, 114; Bryan & Shear Ltd., 74, 120; The Royal Air Force, 111, 137, 141; The Royal Naval Air Station, Lossiemouth, 28, 41, 43; Aerofilms Ltd., 9, 16, 34, 52, 55, 119, 140, 154. South of Scotland Electricity Board, 67, 75; British Aluminium Company, 89. John Dewar Studios provided all the other photographs in the book.

# INTRODUCTION

Scotland for its size has some of the most varied landscape of any country in Europe; it is about 78,000 sq. km in area or only one quarter the size of the British Isles, and its population of five millions is one tenth that of Britain.

Highlands, islands, lowlands and uplands are the fundamental constituents of the Scottish landscape, and the country has a long and fascinating geological history. There are ancient basement rocks such as the Lewisian gneiss of the north-west Highlands; there are granites and schists; there are sandstones from primeval deserts and lavas from phases of volcanic activity. There have been several periods of mountain building which have racked the land; the most significant were the Caledonian, which Scotland shares with Scandinavia and the Hercynian, which is well represented in Britain and on the mainland of Europe. More recently there have been four major phases of glaciation, with re-advances of ice sheets interrupting warmer climates. Glaciers have scoured the mountain valleys, and the ice and meltwater have deposited boulders, clays and sands on lowland areas.

The compelling attraction of sea and coast, mountain and loch, and the colour, brilliance and clarity, gives a particular quality to all Scottish scenery. The weather is variable, the result of Scotland's maritime position and latitudinal location. Scotland lies between 55°N and 60°N, a zone which has the highest frequency of depressions with warm and cold fronts sweeping in from the Atlantic Ocean. But the alternation of sun and rain brings sparkling visibility and intensifies colour values in the landscape. The west coast is warmer in winter than is south-east England; by contrast, the east coast is often in the grip of cold air streams from the Continent. Hence in winter

Scotland has a colder east coast and a milder west coast. When summer comes, temperatures are higher in the south of Scotland than further north, but longer hours of daylight in northerly districts (the 'simmer dim' in Orkney and Shetland) give some compensation for less warmth. Summer weather in Scotland has a bright freshness and is often pleasantly sunny.

Eastern Scotland lies in a rain shadow—in the lee of the hills and mountains and thus the east coast margins from the Borders to Caithness have an annual rainfall of less than 750 mm a year. This moderate rainfall means that there is more sunshine than in the west. The Scottish hills however have heavy rain, and the west Highlands with over 2,000 mm per annum, is the wettest area. This is due to the Atlantic depressions together with the height of the land; rain, mists and cloudiness are the frequent results. If the Scots want the finest scenery they go to the west coast, and if they want sunshine they go to the east. Above 600 m, bare ground is swept by high winds and snow in winter; more than three fifths of the surface of Scotland is mountain and moor, and there are few farmsteads above 200 m.

Scotland's population is one of the most highly urbanized in the world; over 80 per cent of its people live in towns and cities, a tradition which it shares with the Netherlands. Furthermore, most of the population is crammed into the central Lowlands, with $2\frac{1}{2}$ millions in the Clydeside conurbation alone. There early industrialization was associated with commercial expansion and the exploitation of local coal and iron ore resources, which stimulated massive industrial and urban growth. People from the Scottish countryside and from neighbouring Ireland

I

moved into the boom towns. Congestion and neglect caused the degradation of the environment; at the same time, the rapid, but uncoordinated, surge of industries and urban areas resulted in air, soil and water pollution in many parts of the region.

The country and the coast no less than urban areas are now experiencing rapid changes. About 98 per cent of the Scottish land surface is still classified as 'countryside'. The countryside so valuable to man and yet so much taken for granted cannot be retained in a pristine condition without proper care. In Britain, 25 hectares of land on average are made derelict each day. Are Scots, through ignorance or indifference, going to allow the continued deterioration of their incomparable countryside? The reason so many animal species are extinct is not that man has hunted them for food or sport but that he has destroyed their natural habitats. This process may be extended to the human species, and it is logical to consider that without conservation man could destroy his own habitat.

Spectacular increases in mobility and leisure time have brought pressure on recreational land-use of the countryside, not only in the Lowlands, but also in the Highlands and the Uplands. Motor-car ownership has extended the range of exploration of city dwellers, but the motor-car carries with it the overriding need to halt and rest and admire, which is hard to meet in urban surroundings, or even amid intensive agriculture. It is in the forests and hill-land that space can usually be found for car parks and picnic places. At the same time, tourist activity has become much more intense—over four million people visit Scotland each year. The term 'people pollution' has been applied to the impact of man on his environment as a physical and biological force, which can erode and destroy irreplaceable countryside; in much the same way, congestion of housing, over-use of space and lack of facilities produce slums in cities.

The country's natural resources—landscape, air, soil, water and wild life—require assessment first, and secondly, policies of conservation. Conservation has been described as preservation plus wise use. As the organizers of the British programme for European Conservation Year state: 'The countryside has to serve many purposes—as a place to live in, to work in, and to play in. Industry wants part of it for growing food, foresters need it for timber, and townspeople want it for recreation. All these demands must be fitted in, without destroying or spoiling the environment.' Hence planning for degrees of conservation is implicit in many reports, such as the Cairngorm Report. Depredations of the deliberate vandal and the ruthless collector have been added to by sheer numbers of people; some areas require vigorous control to fulfil their function as nature reserves, and there are other places both in the countryside and around built-up areas, where activities must be co-ordinated and channelled, not restrictively but permissively, in accordance with the season and with agricultural practice. Already in the mountain and hill-land, the concept of the multi-purpose use of land is evolving, with leisure-time uses such as climbing, hill walking, ski-ing, deer stalking, fishing and other outdoor pursuits being integrated with forestry and farming.

Measures to manage the environment and improve its quality must be linked with policies of informing and educating people, preferably by involving them actively in planning in both town and country—to get them to enjoy their environment and through appreciating it to feel interested in improving and conserving it. In the countryside people have to be encouraged to explore, to observe, to learn, to record with sketch-book and camera. The Countryside Commission says, 'We don't want people just to gawk at it from their cars as they drive past!' Hence interpretation, or explaining the significance of the countryside to the public, is essential. Most people appreciate the interpretative services and the conservation measures applied by such organizations as the National Trust for Scotland, the Forestry Commission and the Nature Conservancy. Scotland is in fact ahead of most European countries in this pioneer work. The compactness of Scotland and the wealth of interest which every region has to offer makes it well suited to co-ordinated information services. Scots themselves however tend to show a lack of appreciation of their natural and man-made habitats; perhaps the older industrial and run-down urban areas make people oblivious to their outdoor environments. A consequence of technological progress is the residue of obsolescent installations and equipment left by old industries; branch railways are following canals into the realms of industrial archaeology. Derelict transport systems, factory ruins, abandoned mine workings and decaying village communities are some of the scars on the contemporary Scottish scene.

Almost the whole of Scotland is rated as a development area for industrial investment which is desperately needed to provide prosperity for the Scottish people. Factory estates, motorways, new towns, and public and private housing are growing apace and utilizing Scotland's limited resources of arable and pasture land. Oil companies are exploring Scottish waters for oil and have made some rich discoveries that could transform the Scottish economic situation. Developmental pressures are severe in some regions, such as the Firth of Clyde, and diffuse in others. In the Highlands, there is a serious danger that without proper integration, the growing numbers of people may eventually destroy—largely through ignorance—that very heritage of landscape, local life and tradition which so many people come to enjoy.

The purpose of this book is to assist people to know Scotland better, by taking a fresh look at its changing landscapes through oblique aerial photographs, accompanied by a short commentary, thus combining learning with pleasure. It also highlights the pressures which are affecting Scotland from city to countryside, and which are adding new facets to Scottish landscapes.

# SUILVEN; Sutherland

The spectacular scenery of the west coast of Sutherland is symbolized by this superb mountain. Its name is a Gaelic–Norse hybrid, meaning 'pillar fell'.

Ancient Lewisian gneiss forms the basement rock, whose weaknesses have been picked out by the relentless flow of glacier ice and torrents to produce a unique landscape of rock and water. The Torridon sandstone, rich plum red, lies on top of the gneiss in level or gently dipping beds, which are here streaked by snow. The tough sandstone forms the mountain massifs and ridges that have been sculpted into immense buttresses and crags. Suilven (733 m) and its near neighbour, Canisp (849 m) stand above the loch-studded surface like islands in a sea.

Suilven rises 7 kilometres south-east of Lochinver, and it appears as a cone when viewed from west or east, but the summit is in fact a ridge 2·4 km long with three peaks. It is the western peak (*see opposite*) which resembles a giant fang when seen from the coast road north of Lochinver. The hill is usually climbed by the Bealach Mor or Big Pass; and in clear weather commands vistas over mountain, loch and sea to the Outer Hebrides. Snow does not lie long on these mountains close to the Atlantic coast, but the rainfall, 2,000 mm, is substantial.

Ancient Lewisian gneiss

Torridonian sandstone

Quartzite cap

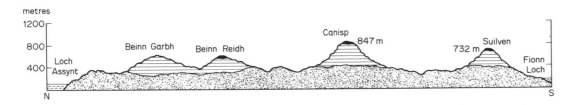

# THE MOOR OF RANNOCH; Argyllshire

This is the biggest desert in Britain—a great granite basin surrounded by mountains of metamorphic and igneous rocks. The moor itself ranges in height from 168 m to over 460 m and is 52 sq. km in extent. In winter time, with its surface snow-clad and its lochs frozen, it resembles a lunar landscape; it recalls a time when an ice sheet flowed outwards from this high barren terrain, feeding valleys around it. Later as ice accumulation lessened, glaciers dumped moraines in and around the basin.

The moor is no dreary brown morass, and although it is unmatched in its desolate extent, it is remarkable for its natural beauty, derived from its tufted surface of thick peat and heather, lochs and islands and its encirclement of clean carved mountains—here the view extends from Ben Lui (*left*) to the peaks of Glen Etive. Loch Tulla sparkles (*left centre*) in winter sun. The railway snakes alongside the Water of Tulla; so villainous was the ground upon which it was built in 1889 that the engineers floated it across on brushwood rafts. Glen Orchy stretches away to the south of the loch. The new Glencoe road strikes across the Moor skirting the twin upswellings of the Black Mount (533 m) (*right centre*), at whose base Lochan nan h-Achlaise is seen. This road was constructed over the western corner of the moor on rafts of concrete. The road parts this lochan from Loch Ba, whose ragged outline is right of centre. From Loch Ba streams run in indeterminate fashion through the peat hags to Loch Laidon (*lower left*). The lochs on the moor feed rivers flowing to the Atlantic and to the North Sea.

The north-east portion of the moor is a nature reserve, providing the habitats associated with blanket bog formation. The Moor of Rannoch offers first-class rough walking for the strong and adequately provisioned, who seek to enjoy the wilderness with its islands wooded with birch and rowan, red deer on the moors and birds swimming on the lochs. There is an abundance of wild flowers, and isolated pine trees, straggling remnants of an ancient forest overwhelmed by peat bog.

# THE GREAT GLEN; Inverness-shire

Glenmore, or the Great Glen of Albin, extends from Loch Linnhe to the Moray Firth. It is a major fault line, disturbed by intense and repeated shattering and forms a spectacular physical feature. This view looks northwards over part of Loch Lochy, towards Loch Oich, with the canal locks at Laggan in the foreground. Loch Ness can be seen in the distance.

The shatter belt of Glenmore is in fact a tear fault; strata have been ripped apart in a displacement estimated as 105 km in length, during which lateral and vertical rock movements have occurred. Occasional earth tremors indicate that the movements are still not over.

The selective action of glaciers has transformed the fault zone into a trough with straight, steep sides. Loch Ness is the giant among the chain of lochs which are situated in the deepest parts of this trough. It is 230 m deep, but only 9 m above sea-level and it is over 39 km long. The lochs have been linked together by the Caledonian Canal, constructed between 1803 and 1822, through which small vessels such as fishing boats and yachts voyage from the North Sea to the Atlantic and thus by-pass the stormy waters of the Pentland Firth. The canal which was surveyed by the Scottish engineer, Thomas Telford, takes up only 35 of Glenmore's 97 km.

The Great Glen is also traversed by the main road from Fort William to Inverness; roadside observatories and viewpoints for monster spotting on Loch Ness encourage travellers to look out for 'Nessie'. It is claimed that there is more than one monster, but very infrequent sightings are reported.

There are fine glens to the west of Glenmore, of which Glen Affric was held to be without equal, but the woodlands have been despoiled and large hydro-electric installations mar the landscape. Only in Glen Strathfarrar and Glen Cannich has interference with the valleys been minimal, and they are as yet removed from the pressures of tourist or industrial development. In other areas superlative natural landscapes have been irreversibly altered by schemes which might have been better integrated with the environment.

# BEN NEVIS; Inverness-shire

Ben Nevis (see also p. 87) is the highest mountain in the British Isles; according to a recent survey it stands 1,349 m above sea-level. Its broad shoulders dominate Fort William on the shores of Loch Linnhe; its southern flanks dip to Glen Nevis, a superb mountain valley, whose gorge has been described as 'Himalayan'.

Westwards Loch Eil, with Corpach on its northern margin, curves towards Glenfinnan; the sun-dappled massif in Lochaber. The county of Inverness has more than fifty peaks over 915 m in height, ten of them in this district.

The massive mountain of Ben Nevis has a stupendous north-east face of rock and ice tall; the summit (*left*) is linked to Carn Mor Dearg and Aonach Beag (both over 1,220 m high) by the snow-corniced ridge in the foreground. Beneath this arête, the 458 m granite wall of Coire Leis drops away. The crags are split into a profusion of ridges and buttresses that draw rock climbers from all parts of Britain. The snow climbing of winter and spring is very severe, long and testing; it should not be attempted by inexpert or ill-equipped climbers.

Ben Nevis can also be ascended by a track, which gives a hill walk to the top, from which a panorama unfolds in clear weather from the Cairngorms to the Hebrides. In 1883 an observatory, the ruins of which may still be traced, was erected on the summit. It is estimated that a drop in the annual average temperature of only 2°C would be sufficient to re-establish glaciers in the highest corries. Weather recordings on the top of Ben Nevis showed that the mean annual temperature was below freezing point, ranging from −4·6°C in February to +4·7°C in July, which is comparable with those of the coast of east-central Greenland. High precipitation much of which falls as snow, and relentless gales, combine to make the climate on Ben Nevis much harsher than such Arctic areas experience.

# LOCH LOMOND; Dunbartonshire and Stirlingshire

Loch Lomond is the most popular natural attraction for tourists in Scotland. This view over the summit of Ben Lomond (974 m) extends southwards to the Clyde valley.

The Highland Boundary fault line crosses the southern end of the loch, where a chain of islands, formed of resistant rocks bordering on softer ones, marks the shatter belt, and from where the abrupt wall of the Highlands is clearly visible. There are remarkable contrasts between the Lowland and Highland sections of the loch. About 10,000 years ago a massive glacier coursed through the valley. The deepest part of the loch is where the ice was most constricted by the mountain sides—the Lowland part of the loch hardly exceeds 30 m in depth, whereas the Highland section is over 183 m deep, far below sea-level. Once free from the enclosing mountains, the Loch Lomond glacier fanned out, depositing earth and rubble in moraines which now partially enclose the southern edge.

There are thirty ice-smoothed islands in the loch; the bigger ones are farmed and the smaller are thickly wooded. Loch Lomond has an area of 70 sq. km and contains 2,640 million m³ of water. As Scotland's water consumption is likely to double within thirty years, Loch Lomond has become a reservoir for a pipeline water grid for the Lowlands. Concrete water pipes 1·52 m in diameter carry the flow as far as Livingston new town; 455,000 m³ a day will be drawn from the loch by a pumping station at Ross Priory on the south-eastern shore. The water is taken from the bed of the loch about 230 m from the pumping station. The height of the loch is regulated by sluices on the river Leven, controlling outfall to the Firth of Clyde,

and a fish-pass has been built to allow the migration of salmon.

The richest and most accessible loch in Scotland for wildlife and varied scenery has thus become a reservoir for central Scotland. The Nature Conservancy won agreement on a maximum water level of 7·9 m O.D., which is 1 m above the present summer minimum and 1·5 m below the winter maximum, which is thought a sufficient safeguard. The higher water level in summer may result in some fine bays being inundated at this season. Naturalists are concerned that the marshes on the south-east margin will be

flooded, thus destroying plant and animal habitats. The reconciling of demand for water with recreational pressures is a major problem. A reduced outflow to the Clyde may intensify pollution of the river Leven. The fisheries of both the Leven and the Clyde were lucrative at one time, but through man's mismanagement are now negligible.

In the holiday season Loch Lomondside is crowded, with cars crawling bumper to bumper along the narrow road on its western shore. A report on recreation and tourism in the region in 1968 revealed that more than one-third of the visitors were day trippers, that 80 per cent or more came by car, and that the increase in active recreation was accompanied by a decline in 'spectator' recreation. The provision of a recreational complex at Balloch, with a marina, motel, caravan and camp site, golf course and picnic area to the west of the river Leven was suggested. These would be linked by a footbridge over the river to indoor facilities, such as a swimming pool and sports hall.

# THE EILDON HILLS; Roxburghshire

The southern uplands are smooth rounded hills carved from Ordovician and Silurian rocks such as mudstones and greywackes. Their weathering rarely yields big boulders or rough outcrops, but rather small flattish stones and screes that contribute to the subdued appearance of the uplands. The occurrence of igneous rocks helps to vary the scenery of the Tweed Basin. Here the Eildon Hills rise a thousand feet above the floor of the Tweed Valley near Melrose.

Isolation gives the Eildon Hills prominence, and makes them a superb vantage-point. There is an indicator at 472 m on the central one of the three summits, marked with places of special interest. From the top Sir Walter Scott could point out forty-three places famous in war and verse. He it was who made the Scottish borders a foremost tourist area in Britain; he set a new value upon tradition and things historic in this verdant countryside, with its wooded hedgerows.

This view shows how managed woodland has an amenity value in screening buildings, enhancing the beauty of the landscape and in providing opportunities for recreation. In France, Italy and the Netherlands, hedgerows are productive, yielding substantial quantities of timber. In Scotland however they are neglected and the countryside is the poorer by their decay. Their power to give shelter and to reduce the wind drift of soil in dry Scottish springs is an invaluable function.

Industrial development in part of the Scott country has been signalled. Between Scott's house at Abbotsford and Darnick 1,000 new houses are being sited. Drift of population from the Borders has been as serious as from the Highlands. Objections to the new developments are strong.

Areas of lower scenic quality than Tweedbank were suggested, in the belief that 'tourists should see this part of the Border countryside as Sir Walter Scott saw it'.

A disused railway crosses the Tweed, by the graceful asymmetrical viaduct (*lower right*). Walkways, cycle tracks or pony trekking routes could well be formed on disused track beds, thus separating such uses from traffic on motor roads, but continuous routeways are broken by the removal of steel girder bridges, which span roads and rivers.

# THE CAIRNGORM MOUNTAINS

The Cairngorms are the largest area of high ground in Britain, with four summits over 1,220 m above sea-level. Ben Macdhui (1,310 m), long considered the highest mountain in the British Isles, and its neighbours Braeriach, Cairntoul and Cairngorm are part of an immense dissected plateau whose northern and eastern faces are rimmed by great corries. The rock type is predominantly red granite, in which quartz crystals, known as Cairngorm gem stones occur.

This view over the shoulder of Benn Mheadhoin (the middle mountain) shows Loch Avon set in a glaciated trough whose massive slopes are mantled by screes and scored by gullies. The Shelter Stone Crag stands at the head of the loch; the valley is traversed by a rough track from Glenmore and Strathavon. There are wastes of frost-shattered boulders on the plateau surface, while solifluction terraces due to freeze-thaw activity are visible on the flanks of the mountains. The panorama extends from the slopes of Ben Macdhui to the slopes of Cairngorm. The Lairig Ghru trenches the plateau from north to south (*top centre*). The scale is such that it is over 3·2 km from the corrie face (*upper right*) to the streams on the plateau surface (*centre*). In the Cairngorms distances are deceptive, and remoteness is enhanced by the wide skies where wind and weather work with an intensity not encountered at lower altitudes.

The corries are vast amphitheatres scooped out by ice action and have rugged rock faces. The Garbh Choire of Braeriach (*upper left*) is 3·2 km long and 3·2 km wide and is an outstanding example of such a corrie. About a quarter of Scotland's corries contain a loch, and one of the biggest is Loch Coire-an-Lochan of Braeriach. There are oppor-tunities for ski-ing in the smoother corries, such as Coire Cas on Cairngorm, which holds snow well, and may carry snowfields throughout the year. Recurrent flash floods devastate the slopes so that roads and other installations require careful siting. The ski road to Coire Cas has been much improved since its initial alignment.

Intensive development of ski-facilities has led to destruction of plant cover and to the erosion of the loose grits and screes along ski tows and paths; the mountain vegetation is like a threadbare carpet that is easily worn away. Attempts to plant grass to consolidate the surface are being made, and the route from the top chairlift station to the summit of Cairngorm has been diverted. Tourists should have a map and compass and not wander far from the top without adequate clothing and food. Distant parts of the high plateau between Cairngorm and Ben Macdhui are now much more accessible to hill walkers and research has started on the effects which the impact of more people is having on the natural environment.

Glenmore National Forest Park is now famous as a centre for outdoor activities; Loch Morlich, with its sandy beach, is an attractive place for dinghy sailing, while near by there is a caravan and camping ground and youth hostel. Flocks of tourists come for walking and rock climbing, and for ski-ing in winter. The Cairngorm Nature Reserve on the western massif is over 25,600 ha in area. There arctic-alpine plants, native pine forest and a wealth of wild animals and birds are protected. The reindeer has been introduced to the region, and the osprey has been re-established in the foothills.

# PLOCKTON, LOCH CARRON;
# Wester Ross

High above Plockton, the eye sweeps eastwards across Loch Carron, studded with islands, to the narrows at Strome Ferry. On the horizon the snow-clad outline of the Fannich mountains in central Ross shows in winter grandeur.

Loch Carron is a highland fjord; glaciers flowed out radially from the mountain core where altitude and heavy snowfall aided ice accumulation. The sea-lochs occupy valleys powerfully eroded by ice, and are just like other loch-filled rock basins, except that they have been inundated by salt water and not by fresh. Where the valleys widened out, the glaciers had less capacity to cut and deepen; islands often appear in such places.

Most of the big sea-lochs are composed of more than one rock basin, and the rock barriers between frequently coincide with narrows which provide convenient points for ferry crossings as at Ballachulish, Kylesku or here at Strome. Contrary to widely held opinion, the deepest parts of Scottish sea-lochs tend to be towards their seaward ends, from which points the water becomes much shallower, and there is a threshold or sill of solid rock. The waters of Loch Carron merge into the Inner Sound which separates Skye from the mainland.

Plockton itself is a fishing village on the Balmacara estate, which is a property of the National Trust for Scotland. It is a holiday and stop-over place for tourists. The railway which runs in sinuous curves along the south shore of the loch was opened to Kyle of Lochalsh in 1897. The journey, 132 km from Inverness, is well worth making.

The line was spared closure and crosses superb country, giving the traveller a transect of Highland Scotland. Strome is a vital link in the emerging concept of a scenic west Highland tourist route. But car ferries, inadequate for heavy summer traffic, caused long and temper-fraying delays there. A new road, 12 km long, by-passing the ferry has been constructed, but has encountered persistent landslides, so that a section has been tunnelled—an expedient by no means uncommon in Norway or Switzerland, but unprecedented on a main road in Highland Scotland.

# LOCH TAY; Perthshire

The county of Perth has extraordinary richness and variety in its landscapes. Loch Tay begins where Glen Lochay and Glen Dochart come together, and where glaciers moving along these valleys combined to gouge out a rock basin over 150 m deep. The loch itself is over 24 km long and extends to over 26 sq. km in area.

The majority of the big Highland lochs are much longer than they are broad, and have been termed 'ribbon lakes'. Loch Tay is like Lochs Ness and Morar in that it fills a huge rock basin lying within faulted and shattered belts of rock, which assisted glacial erosion.

About 10,000 years ago the Tay and its neighbouring valleys were deeply laden with ice, which spilt over cols and broke through interconnecting gaps as glaciers moved out from the Grampians to lower levels. High-level passages have thus been cut at angles to the trend of the dominant valleys. Lochan na Lairige (*upper centre*), which is now a reservoir for hydro-electricity, is situated in such a gap between Glen Lyon and Loch Tay.

Infilling of the loch is occurring at Killin (*lower centre*) which is a popular village for tourists. The rivers are dumping spreads of sand and gravel in delta forms extending out into the loch.

Loch Tay empties to the river Tay, which is said to carry the largest volume of water of any river in Britain and is renowned for its salmon fishing. It is overlooked on the north side by Ben Lawers (1,211 m), Perthshire's highest summit, which is in the possession of the National Trust for Scotland. The main road follows this shore, from which a hill route branches to a car park and information centre. This mountain property covers 3,200 ha and public access is allowed at all times. The arctic-alpine plants of the corries are protected because of their botanical interest —visitors should come to admire and to learn, but may not collect specimens of this rare flora. There are nature trails and an impressive ridge walk from Ben Ghlas to Ben Lawers. In winter the mountain is a ski-ing ground; the Scottish Ski Club Hut in Coire Odhar is 3·2 km from the car park.

Competition for water space on Loch Tay has shown that sailing and fishing can exist together. Loch Earn to the south is a recognized centre for water ski-ing and motor boating. However the noise of these sports conflicts with fishing and other leisure activities, so some separation of activities is desirable.

# THE STORR; Isle of Skye

Large-scale landslides are the most dramatic evidence of insecure rock structure. An impressive example occurs in the peninsula of Trotternish in the north of Skye where, beneath an imposing escarpment over 610 m high, which is marked by the Storr and Quiraing, huge masses of basalt have collapsed. The stepped hillsides are prone to landslips because of the slippery shales and clays underlying the lava flows. The slumped debris lies in a belt up to 0·8 km wide in a series of tilted blocks and fantastic rock pinnacles interspersed with tiny lochans and wet hollows.

Land slipping was common in late glacial times, owing to the steepening of slopes, torn by the passage of glaciers. The scale may vary from mere scars on a hillside to huge chutes of debris, as on the north coast of Arran, and in the islands of Eigg and Raasay. The process is helped by heavy rainfall and frost action.

The Storr (*right*) has crags over 720 m in height, and the extraordinary rock needle (*left centre*) is the famous 'Old Man of Storr', a lava spine 49 m high, which is backed by the escarpment.

Loch Leatham is seen beyond the Old Man of Storr; the loch is a hydro-electric reservoir with a dam at its seaward outfall to the Sound of Raasay. Across the low saddle lies the harbour of Portree, the administrative and shopping centre of Skye.

Thirty-two kilometres to the south, the Cuillins rise in majesty above a bank of cloud haze. Marsco dips to Glen Sligachan; the principal range with Sgurr nan Gillean (the peak of the lads) continues in linking aretes to Sgurr Alasdair, the highest mountain on the island.

# GLENCOE; Argyllshire

Glencoe is known to thousands of travellers who speed through it on the 'New Road', which dates from 1935, and who gaze through windscreen wipers at the soaring crags and corries swirling in mist. The road (*lower left*) skirts the Moor of Rannoch to approach Glencoe from the south-east. The triangular massif of Buachaille Etive Mor, 'the great herdsman of Etive' (1,020 m) (*left centre*), stands watch over the entrance to the glen. This mountain, carved from rhyolite, is the most popular rock-climbing ground in Scotland and is only 2½ hours by car from Glasgow. The Crowberry Tower and numerous gullies and pinnacles thrill the competent mountaineer on a winter's day such as this, when the peak casts deep shadows across the valley. A trench connecting with Glen Etive separates the peak from its smaller neighbour, Buachaille Etive Beag (925 m). Then comes Bidean nam Bian (1,150 m) the highest mountain in Argyll, which walls in Glencoe on the south. It has nine tops, the most famous of which are the Three Sisters (Beinn Fhada, Gearr Aonach and Aonach Dubh), and three vast corries. The lost valley, a mountain sanctuary, is encircled by the crags of Bidean. A roadside viewpoint in the middle of the defile offers impressive vistas of the Three Sisters. Here the river Coe flows westwards over foaming cascades and through clear pools to enter Loch Achtriochtan.

The glen itself is an ice-worn valley, mantled with screes and debris from the mountains. Whereas the north-facing slopes are steep and rocky, the south-facing ones sweep down almost uninterrupted from watershed to valley floor. The peaty flats of the lower pass are in sharp contrast with the towering precipices and waterfalls around them. This was the land of the massacre of the MacDonalds in 1692.

24

This episode, described as political murder, is one of the stains on Scottish history.

On the north flank is the Aonach Eagach or notched ridge, which is 10 km in length and over 910 m high; the winter-time traverse is as arduous as that of an Alpine arête. From the summits the eye lifts to snow-streaked peaks packed in close array and trenched by ravines. In the far distance on this photograph is Ben More on the island of Mull.

The mountains on both sides of Glencoe belong to the National Trust for Scotland, which has experimented here in countryside care with its litter disposal systems and campaigns.

25

# THE GREY MARE'S TAIL; Dumfriesshire

The Grey Mare's Tail is a splendid waterfall, over 60 m high formed by the Tail Burn as it drops from Loch Skene to meet the Moffat Water. This stream is followed by the A708 road from Selkirk to Moffat via St. Mary's Loch. The difference in level between the main valley and the hanging valley above is 210 m. Hanging valleys are found widely in Scottish hill-country, and owe their form to the deepening of the major valley by the passage of a glacier. Once the ice retreated, streams on the hillsides spilt down to the new valley floor in cascades. The slopes are torn by gullies and scars marking the slipping of rock waste after heavy rain and frost or snow melt.

Over 800 ha of land around the waterfall were purchased by the National Trust for Scotland in 1962. Warning notices point out that the path skirting the ravine is a dangerous one, and must be negotiated with every care. Other waterfall and gorge areas are also protected by the National Trust. Among these are the Falls of Glomach in Kintail, which are difficult of access being reached only on foot, and the Corrieshalloch gorge through which the waters of the Falls of Measach flow to Loch Broom, near the main road to Ullapool.

Some gorges have been obscured by hydro-electric dams, as at Kilmorack in the Beauly valley, and at the eastern end of Loch Tummel. Both gorges and waterfalls are tourist magnets, but their scale is almost in proportion to their remoteness. Eas-Coul-Aulin, a waterfall in wild and roadless country in Sutherland, is more than twice the height of Niagara Falls; it is a magnificent spectacle in spate, but may be reached only on foot or by boat.

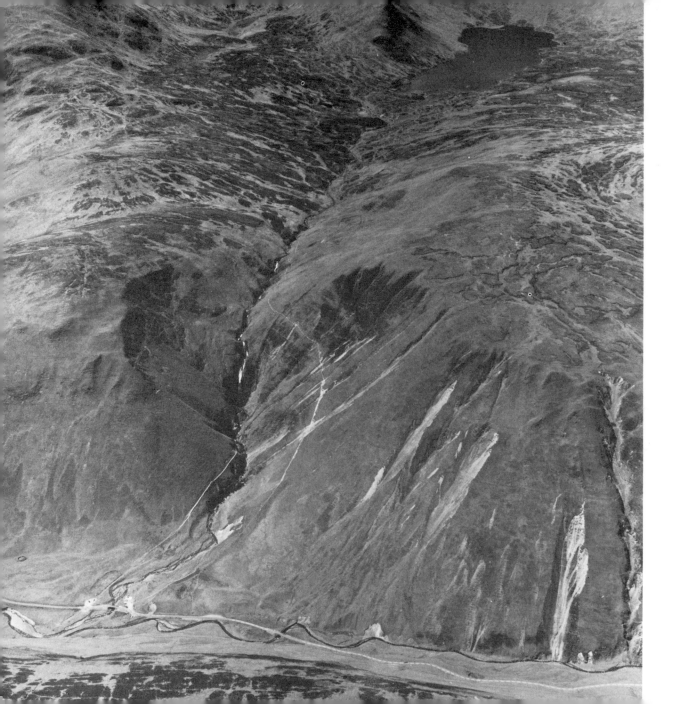

27

# THE RIVER SPEY; Morayshire

Shingle beaches, spits and shoals fringe the mouth of the Spey, the second largest river in Scotland. Rising in the Grampians and flowing through Badenoch and the foothills of the Cairngorms to enter Strathspey, and thus to the Moray Firth, the river has slow meandering reaches interrupted by constricted boulder-strewn stretches, features which it shares with the Tay and the Dee.

Often old valleys dating back to the Ice Age or earlier are hidden beneath rock debris, deposited by glaciers and the streams which flowed from them. Present-day rivers have either found their former valleys and cleared a way through them, or else have cut new valleys for themselves; so rocky gorges alternate with wider valley tracts. Changes in course and downcutting by the river have planed the sands and gravels of the valley into terraces: a sinuous terrace rimmed by a road to the right of centre on the photograph shows clearly. The steep terrace edges are either left forested or uncultivated, whereas the flat surfaces provide useful soils for cultivation.

The bed of the river is braided, dividing into channels interspersed with shoals. The headwaters of the Spey and its tributaries are prone to floods: such was the immensity of the great floods of 1829 that parts of the valley became temporary lakes. In 1956, more than 600 ha of fertile haughland in Moray were covered with coarse gravel as a result of inundation.

The westwards drift of wind and tide deflects the mouth of the Spey, impeding the passage of flood water. Although the spit is broken at times of flood it has also been breached artificially, the most recent occasion being in 1962. At the current rate of growth another channel will be necessary in the 1980s.

There have also been problems in bridging the river. The viaduct on the branchline railway between Elgin and the Banffshire coast can be seen, but many places in Strathspey show by the 'boat' place-names (Boat of Insh, Boat of Garten) where ferries once plied.

# THE ISLE OF ARRAN; Buteshire

The county of Bute is one of three Scottish counties consisting solely of islands. Arran, 23 km by ferry from the Ayrshire coast, is *par excellence* a holiday island. The northern half with its glens and mountains is scenically the outstanding region. Brodick, on the eastern side, is the largest town and its pier is served by Clyde steamers. From the sweep of Brodick bay, Goatfell 876 m, the highest mountain on Arran, soars behind Brodick Castle; the whole estate is in the care of the National Trust for Scotland.

From the summit ridges of Arran, magnificent views extend over the Firth of Clyde in which the island is set. To the north, beyond the low-lying island of Bute, stand the rugged hills of Cowal; to the west, the long peninsula of Kintyre points towards Ireland. For the walker and climber, May, June and September often bring drier weather than the height of summer.

The Highland problem begins in Arran: across the Firth, the industrial expansion of Ayrshire and Renfrewshire lures people away—indeed the rate of de-population is more rapid than in the Highland region. Yet Arran is not part of the political Highlands—Bute is not a crofting county; it has no benefits from the Highlands and Islands Development Board. On the other hand Arran is certainly not Lowland in character. The stage has been reached where reports ask how many people are required to keep the transport and other services viable: the present population is about 3,000 people.

A new pier and car ferry operated in 1970 to Brodick as part of the programme to improve the services for the car tourist. A 90 km road encircles the island, linking together delightful villages, but unlike Scandinavia, there are no inter-island ferries, and no bridge links Bute to encourage island hopping. Arran has the natural advantage of matchless scenery, and already holiday and tourist facilities are expanding. Brodick has added sea angling to the multitude of activities which the island has to offer the visitor, and Arran is growing in popularity with school and university parties which come for geological and other field studies from all over Britain

# GLEN DOCHART; Perthshire

Near Crianlarich, the waters of Loch Dochart and Loch Tubhair spread across the valley floor. The lochs lie at the foot of the peaks of Ben More (1,259 m) and Stobinian (1,252 m), left, which face Stob Garbh (1,032 m) and Cruach Ardrain across a hanging valley. These mountains are landmarks throughout the Grampians.

The Benmore burn descends swiftly to the main valley and has strewn coarse alluvial deposits across Glen Dochart, infilling a former lake, already partly divided by the extensive moraine, of considerable extent, thus making two lochs out of one. Several former lakes have been filled up by such deposition, as in Strathglass and in the Upper Spey valley.

The Benmore deposits take the form of an alluvial fan. Such features develop where streams wash debris off hill-slopes, and they are a significant addition to farm land, offering free-draining, if stony, soil, at the margins of Scottish lochs. Over-grazing and moor-burning have accelerated erosion on hill-land; the down-slope movement of loose material has thus been encouraged by man's activities. If this sequence should remain unchecked, vast areas of bare infertile rock would be left on the hillsides, and huge amounts of coarse debris would accumulate in the valleys. Bracken (*Pteridium aquilinum*), a notorious invader of hill-pasture, has some advantages in stabilizing rock waste, but has no nutritional value for stock, and drives out nourishing grasses.

The farms on the alluvial fan are Port Nellan and Benmore, from which a hill-pass or 'bealach' leads through the mountains to the Braes of Balqhidder, the homeland of the MacGregors. Shelter belts protect the steadings and ground is being prepared for further afforestation. Reconciling the claims of the hill-farmer and the forester for use of the moorland is a recurring problem, but one solution is to integrate a proportion of forestry with hill-farming.

# AILSA CRAIG; Ayrshire

Like a fortress sentinel, the island of Ailsa Craig rises sheer to a height of 340 m at the entrance to the Firth of Clyde. It is composed of intrusive igneous rock, and the passage of ice in glacial times carried stones and boulders plucked from the island as far as Lancashire, South Wales and Ireland—a distance in excess of 480 km.

Ailsa Craig is 3·2 km in circumference and is about 19 km off the Ayrshire coast from Girvan. A lighthouse and an ancient ruined castle are situated on the island, whose finely speckled 'microgranite' is quarried for the manufacture of curling stones, with which the 'Roaring Game' is played. Curling is a winter sport, requiring an ice rink, and Scotland has exported the game to Canada and Scandinavia, which now in return give Scots players stern competition in international matches.

Colonies of seabirds, especially gannets and puffins, breed unmolested on Ailsa Craig, which is affectionately known as 'Paddy's Milestone' lying as it does halfway between Glasgow and Belfast in Ireland. For travellers by sea or air, it is often their first introduction to Scotland's 787 islands.

# THE BASS ROCK; East Lothian

This self-assertive landmark lies off the coast from North Berwick. The steepness of its sides makes it appear taller than its 107 m). The island is about 1·6 km in circumference, and its tough igneous rocks are the last link in a chain of volcanic masses that stretch across central Scotland. The rock's form has been sharpened by ice movement, as well as by the ceaseless battering of wave, wind and tide. There is a natural fissure opening out into an east to west cavern.

The Bass Rock is accessible only from the landing-place at the south corner (*left*), from which a stepped path leads to the lighthouse. A cliff-top route connects the lighthouse with its foghorn, set to blast its warning into the Forth estuary. The Bass Rock has also been a hermitage, a prison and a fortress, and it figures in stories of adventure such as R. L. Stevenson's *Catriona*.

Beyond the rock, more islands appear like ships sailing in line astern. The East Lothian shore with its delectable beaches, prosperous agriculture and well-tended towns stretches westwards. North Berwick Law (187 m) on the left is a fine vantage-point for studying both the coastline and the islands. There are regular trips by motor boat from North Berwick round the rock to watch the nesting sea-birds which crowd its cliffs; foremost among them is the gannet which derives its Latin name, *Sula bassana*, from this island. It is known locally as the Solan goose. Occasional landings on the Bass Rock are permitted for groups of visitors.

# ISLE OF JURA; Argyllshire

Jura is one of Scotland's big islands, though less well-known and visited than its neighbour Islay (*upper right*). This view looks south to the long inlet of Loch Tarbert, which almost divides the island in half. Beyond rise the shapely Paps of Jura, the highest of which is 770 m above the sea. These upstanding mountains are composed of quartzite which resists weathering and in good visibility they are prominent landmarks from the mainland and from near-by islands. Jura is about 45 km long and 13 km broad.

The island is linked by ferry to Port Askaig in Islay, and its village Craighouse in the south east corner is served by steamer from west Loch Tarbert in Kintyre.

Abandoned cliffs with caves and stacks, now out of reach of the sea, line the west coast; these features are seen at the margin of smooth platforms, which reach their maximum development in Jura, Islay and Mull. The smoothed surfaces (*left*) stand 30–33 m above sea-level, and are overlain by 'raised beach' gravels—shingle spreads of quartz pebbles in patterns of curving lines. The ridges are more pronounced here than anywhere else in Scotland, and they support little plant cover.

Nearer the sea at a height of 8 m or so, another old beach is discernible. Discussing these land forms in *The Evolution of Scotland's Scenery*, J. B. Sissons writes:

The abandoned cliffs and wave cut platforms often appear remarkably fresh, and there is no difficulty in visualising the waves breaking against the former shore.

The development of these 'raised beaches' has been attributed to changing sea-levels and to the warping of the land surface both before and since glaciation. In the west Highlands and islands, raised beaches with their shell sands have provided almost the only available flat land for settlement and route-ways, as well as some depth of soil for agriculture. Jura is, however, given over largely to sporting estates, and the west coast does not appear to have been settled in historic times.

# BALRANALD; North Uist, Inverness-shire

Sand-dune terrain has a particularly dynamic quality. Narrow belts of dunes are found along many parts of the Scottish coast from Ayrshire to East Lothian. Spreads of sand cover extensive areas as at Tentsmuir in East Fife, and around Balnakiel Bay in Sutherland. In North Uist (*see opposite*) blown sand has formed sandy plains or 'machair' between the coastal dune margin and the peat moors and hills of the interior. The lime-rich sands, derived from sea shells, have contributed much to the fertility of islands, such as Tiree, and they occur almost continuously on the west coast of the Outer Hebrides. There cattle are pastured on the machair, which is made brilliant by the wild flowers and lush grass of early summer. In North Uist crofters cultivate the machair in runrig, long narrow strips scattered in open fields; the shell sands are also carried to the peaty soil areas as fertilizer. Bulb growing is successful in Tiree, and here in North Uist pilot schemes have been started.

Beaches of fine pinkish sand are attractive for bathing, but other forms of land-use such as golf courses and military training grounds are also encountered in dune areas in Scotland. Balranald itself is part of a nature reserve managed by the Royal Society for the Protection of Birds and is especially noted for the little tern.

Wide sandy beaches exposed at low tide present ample loose material for strong winds to sweep inland. Sand craters are torn by gales. The consequences of grazing, and other interference with vegetation are still far from fully understood. Coastal sands attract many visitors but they are especially vulnerable to the pressure of their feet. Trampling erodes sandy wastes, giving dust storms when winds are strong; too many people moving over dunes destroy marram grass and other plants. With protection, recovery of the vegetation is complete within four years. In East Lothian, protective brushwood and grass are being established to counteract wind erosion and to stabilize dunes on the coast.

Beaches are prone to pollution, either from oil or other spillage at sea, or from effluent from towns and cities. Many communities are finding sewage disposal an unpleasantly neglected problem. The Firth of Forth had 250 million litres of untreated waste from Edinburgh daily pumped into it until a sewage treatment plant was built recently. Scotland's coastline has been spared serious oil pollution but oil production off-shore requires strict control.

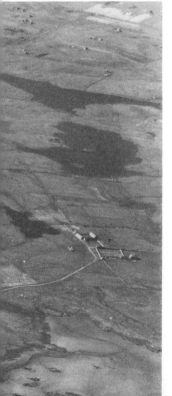

# FINDHORN BAY; Morayshire

Findhorn is a modest resort and fishing village on the east side of Findhorn Bay, where the river of that name enters the Moray Firth. Two previous villages have vanished, engulfed by sands and floods in the eighteenth century. Prior to this, Findhorn was the chief fishing port and harbour of Moray.

A westerly coastwise drift, backed by wind and tide, has built up a bar which nearly encloses Findhorn Bay, making it a lagoon for pleasure sailing. Close at hand are bathing beaches, sprinkled with huts and a caravan site. The demand for water space for recreation is soaring. By far the most popular picnic and play places for Scots have water features.

Westwards, the Culbin Sands extend to over 1,480 ha and attain over 31 m in height. The low rainfall of the Laigh of Moray (less than 600 mm per annum) and strong winds picking up sand from the beaches have helped to develop the greatest spread of blown sands in Scotland. The Barony of Culbin was already affected by sand drift when a disastrous sandstorm overwhelmed it in 1694. Marram grass uprooted from the dunes had been used to thatch houses—a practice which was thereupon prohibited by the Scots parliament. Today the only sign of once-fertile farmland, where grain and fruit ripened to perfection in the long hours of sunshine, are the plough furrows and cart tracks occasionally revealed when the wind moves the sands.

In 1922, the Forestry Commission took over the Culbin Sands, and began a policy of stabilizing and reclaiming the dunes by thatching the sands with birch branches, so that trees, such as the Scots and Corsican pine, could be planted. The effects of wind erosion are now less dramatic, but dust storms are not uncommon in dry springs, when the top soil may be substantially removed. The river Findhorn in flood carries vast quantities of sand and silt to the sea which are swept into the beaches, bars and spits which fringe the coast of the Moray Firth.

# CHANONRY POINT; Ross and Cromarty

Near Fortrose on the south shore of the Black Isle, this shapely peninsula of elevated shingle ridges, known as Chanonry Point projects into the Moray Firth. It approaches to within almost a mile of the similar peninsula on the opposite side, on which Fort George is built.

The Black Isle is neither black nor an island. The description is derived from its snow-free, or 'black' ground in winter. It is in fact a large peninsula which juts out between two arms of the Moray Firth—the Cromarty Firth to the north and the Beauly Firth to the south. The nearest town is Fortrose, which by virtue of its easterly position is one of the driest and sunniest places in Scotland. Chanonry is the old name for Fortrose, which was in the Canonry of Ross.

The lighthouse commands an extensive view of the waters and shores of the Moray Firth. It was built on the point in 1846, at a cost of £3,500; the engineer was Alan Stevenson, uncle of the author Robert Louis Stevenson. The tower is 13 m high and the light has a range of 18 km. The Scottish lighthouses are in the control of the Commissioners of the Northern Lights, who maintain seventy manned lighthouses and over 100 automatic lights on the coast of Scotland and the Isle of Man.

Chanonry Point has been formed by longshore drift building up debris from wave abrasion against the shoreline. Spits usually bend landwards at their tips and are characteristic of emerging coasts due to a rising land surface or falling sea-level. Groynes and other protective works are often required to hold the loose beach material in place.

# STAFFA; Inner Hebrides

This small uninhabited island of the Inner Hebrides is passed each weekday in summer by the mail steamer from Oban to Iona. Staffa is only 28 ha in extent, but it is celebrated for its extraordinary caves in basalt formations; tertiary lavas have cooled into hexagonal columns with strong vertical joints which have been rent by the hammer blows of Atlantic storm waves over aeons of time. The best known is Fingal's Cave (*far right*); it is over 69 m in length and its roof is more than 18 m above sea-level. The columnar structure shows clearly on the Great Face (*right centre*); the immense chasm directly in view is the Boat Cave, and McKinnon's Cave is located to the west of Port an Fhasgaidh, the rocky embayment (*left centre*). The Clam Shell Cave, where the landing-place is located and from which a causeway leads to Fingal's Cave, is situated on the east side of the island and is concealed from view. The lava plateau of north-west Mull forms the background.

Staffa was first brought to people's attention in 1772 by the explorer, Sir Joseph Banks, who passed it on his way to Iceland. Pennant's *Tour in Scotland* written in 1774 gives the earliest description of the island. It was not long before the impressiveness of its structure and gaping chasms was drawing visitors from afar, especially after steamboat trips began in the 1820s. It has been visited and written about by a host of famous tourists—Scott, Turner, Tennyson and Mendelssohn, whose overture, *The Hebrides*, in which he sought to capture the surge of waves breaking and the musical flow of sea water, was inspired by Fingal's Cave.

Uninhabited for more than a century, Staffa is one of the many 'deserted islands' of Scotland. It is used for sheep grazing in summer. The Hebrides have an unrealized potential for cruising and sailing, with the reward of making landfalls in remote and beautiful places.

# FORESTRY; Minard Forest, Argyllshire

A basic question is whether hill-farming or forestry is the most productive land-use in the uplands of Scotland. Only 10 per cent of the land surface is forested, compared with 18 per cent in Belgium, and 25 per cent in West Germany. The Forestry Commission, a state agency, manages areas from Kircudbright to Sutherland amounting to 680,000 hectares about half of which is forested, and it plants up to 20,000 ha a year.

Minard Forest (*see opposite*) on the western shores of Loch Fyne is part of the larger Kilmichael Forest. It is one of many afforested areas in the Western Conservancy, of which the Argyll National Forest Park which encompasses Loch Eck north of Dunoon, is also part.

Softwoods from coniferous trees are most in demand. Sitka spruce (*Picea sitchensis*) discovered in Alaska by the Scottish botanist, Archibald Menzies, is the most widely planted tree in the heavy rainfall and peaty soils of the west Highlands. Norway spruce is second, followed by Lodge pole pine, Scots pine, hybrid larch and Douglas fir. Planting is varied to take account of soil and aspect while increasing attention is paid to colour and form by introducing hardwoods, mainly oak and beech, at roadsides or picnic points.

Cultivation is accomplished by giant ploughs, which cut ditches: fertilizers stimulate tree growth and counteract mineral deficiencies in the soil. The Commission employs about 4,500 men in Scotland who are housed in forest villages, which are a recent and distinctive settlement feature. A tree-planting-cutting cycle has not yet been established: softwoods take from fifty to seventy years to reach maturity, but do become productive after fifteen to twenty years when plantations are thinned.

Forestry is facing changing markets and techniques; the sale of pit-props is much reduced, but the demand for pulp wood is soaring, although Scottish timber products cannot compete with those of Canada or Scandinavia on a cost basis. To haul the one million tonnes of timber sold annually, the Commission had to build about 160 km of forest road. There are the risks of storm damage (a volume equivalent to the annual output was blown down in the west of Scotland in January 1968) and of fire.

The Commission's policies of conservation of wild life, and the clothing of bare hill-slopes and moors with forest have brought great advantages to Scotland. The recreational functions of forests may outweigh commercial considerations in areas where 'the Forestry Commission can offer an increasingly town based society greater opportunity to enjoy the countryside and access to more space'. This observation is amply supported wherever the Commission has provided tourist facilities, access and information, as in the National Forest Parks, of which there are five in Scotland. It also runs camping sites, at Ardgartan near Arrochar, and at Glenmore in the Cairngorms and other locations. The forest trails, parking and picnic places, with their bench seats and tables are thoroughly commendable endeavours, particularly when they are adequately supervised and serviced.

# INVERPOLLY FOREST; Ross and Cromarty

Inverpolly is a wilderness lying to the north of Ullapool in Wester Ross. 'Forest' is a misnomer because woodland is almost entirely absent—a deer forest in the Highlands is a sporting estate. Remote and scarcely inhabited, Inverpolly is now a nature reserve of about 10,920 ha and has been in the care of the Nature Conservancy since 1962.

The loch-scattered moorland offers a diversity of

habitats—lochs, streams, moor, birch-hazel woods, screes and peat moss. The re-establishment of a sub-arctic flora is being investigated. Part of Inverpolly is grazed by the ubiquitous Cheviot sheep, but the native fauna include wild cats, pine marten, red and roe deer.

Geologically, the Moine Thrust Zone is exposed on the eastern edge of the forest. The largest of a chain of lochs—Loch Lurgain and Loch Bad a' Ghaill (*centre*) are surrounded by well-known mountains. Cul Mor (847 m) (*upper left*) and Cul Beag (770 m) (*upper centre*) whose Torridonian sandstone has a protective capping of quartzite, are seen beside Loch Sionascaig (*left*). From the shore of Loch Lurgain, Stac Pollaidh (717 m) rises to a long summit ridge fretted into pinnacles; its flanks are seamed with gullies. Beinn an Eoin, an outlier of Ben More Coigach, borders the loch to the south. At Knockan on the east side of Inverpolly, a viewpoint and car park have been constructed, with an indicator identifying the main features of the landscape; tourists can relax here, and look at the scenery without obstruction to other road traffic. In *Highland Landscape*, W. H. Murray praises Inverpolly as an area of outstanding quality:

When the sky is bright, the lochs scintillate, brilliantly blue, and above them the wild hills rise stark. When the sky is heavy and grey mists twist among the mountain spires, they glint whitely or lie black and fathomless. The scene is never without beauty, weird or brilliant as the skies dictate.

The lochs fill hollows in Lewisian gneiss, one of Europe's oldest rocks, bared by ice, which gives way to an exciting coastline of bays and peninsulas. A single-track road to Achiltibuie follows Loch Lurgain, while a branch continues over hair-raising bends and gradients to Lochinver.

# CROFTING; Lewis, Ross and Cromarty

A high proportion of rough rocky terrain, combined with an excessive rainfall and strong winds, makes farming difficult in the western Highlands and Islands. Hill-farming is one response, crofting is another. There are seven crofting counties from Argyll to Shetland, with 19,000 crofts producing about a quarter of the total agricultural output of the area. A crofter either pays rent of not more than £50 or manages less than 30 ha in districts which suffer from comparative isolation and limited land resources.

Crofting is essentially part-time. A croft, or holding, consists of a little arable land plus some hill grazing, giving a basic income, which may be supplemented by earnings from fishing, forestry, accommodating tourists, shop keeping or as here on the west coast of Lewis by tweed making.

There are about 16,000 crofters in Highland Scotland, many of whom have a distinctive cultural background and are Gaelic speaking. In 1955, the Crofters' Commission was established to reorganize and develop crofting, through the re-allocation of land and the administration of grants and loans. Crofting townships are typically located by coast or lochside; this view shows the ice-scoured rocks with pockets of wet peat, tilled as 'lazy beds' by ditching; near the sea the shell sand of the beaches provides 'machair' for grazing and some cultivation.

In spite of financial help to improve holdings and to reseed grazing, crofting faces serious problems. Lewis lost 11 per cent of its people between 1951–61, principally by emigration which indicates that all is not well with the crofting counties. The position is worse where there are limited opportunities for additional work such as the weaving of Harris tweed. The Highland and Island Development Board set up in 1965 has already transformed island economies, such as Scalpay, Harris, by its promotion of local fisheries. In Wester Ross and elsewhere, bed and breakfast for tourists is making a worthwhile addition to income. The growth of tourism poses the question 'How can changes come to the crofting counties without destroying a way of life?' Resource assessment and imaginative planning are prerequisites of tourist development for the 'Gaelteachd'. The problem of under-sized farm units is shared by other European agricultural systems as is the impact of tourism on remote and unspoiled places.

# LOCH KATRINE; Perthshire

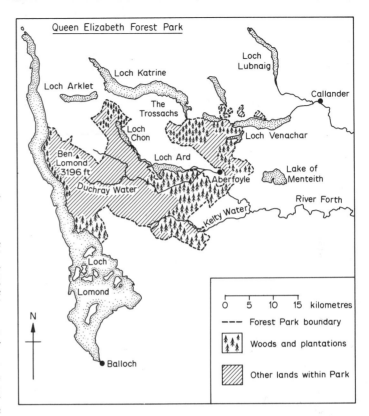

The Trossachs are a superb blend of mountain, wood and loch running westwards from Callander towards Loch Lomond. The name is taken from the wooded defile between Loch Achray and Loch Katrine (*see opposite*) which is one of the most celebrated literary beauty spots in Britain. The Trossachs now have a regional significance, their fame owing much to Sir Walter Scott's *The Lady of the Lake* and *Rob Roy* which introduced the district to tourists.

Loch Katrine is ringed by hills, the most prominent of which is rocky Ben Venue (730 m) (*left*). The panorama from the tops is out of all proportion to their height and stretches from Arran to the Cairngorms and the Firth of Forth.

It is from Loch Katrine and its neighbouring lochs, which together hold 100,800 million litres, that Glasgow draws its water supply, through tunnels and aqueducts first opened in 1855. The purity of the water is unsurpassed in Britain. The loch has been raised twice by skilful engineering, but its 'silver strand' and some islands have been inundated. The steamer, *Sir Walter Scott*, sails its waters in summer—a pleasurable alternative for the motorist, as far too few Scottish lochs may be explored in this way. At the pier there is a parking place and tea room which are commendably restrained in design and compatible with the environment.

The 'Highlands in miniature', with walks and picnic places, on the margin of the Lowlands, have intense usage by tourists and day visitors from urban central Scotland, increasing yearly. The Trossachs are now part of the Queen Elizabeth Forest Park, which commemorates the Coronation. Major timber-producing coniferous forests have been well integrated with a landscape of outstanding natural beauty, and a pleasing planting of species gives colour variation and allows open views.

It is impossible in such a superlative area of scenic beauty for man to improve upon nature. Hence watchfulness is required so that no intrusions of regimented plantations or of disfiguring pylons are permitted. In Scotland popular views to tempt the photographer are too often spoiled by telephone and power lines erected without regard to landscape value.

The Trossachs may be reached either from Callander or by the Duke's Road from Aberfoyle.

53

# HILL-FARMING; Glen Devon, Perthshire

Over 70 per cent of Scotland's land surface consists of rough moorland of little or no value to the farmer. Above 305 m conditions are impossible for intensive agriculture, with heavy rainfall, low temperatures, bare rock and acid soils. Stock rearing has become the predominant activity of the better hill-lands. The lava plateaux of the central Lowlands and the southern Uplands are vast expanses of rolling hills, covered with short grass and heather, rising to over 610 m and are interlaced with narrow valleys and wandering streams. There are also forestry plantations and the valleys with their reservoirs are sources of water.

This view of Glen Devon in the Ochil Hills shows the upland valleys in which stand hill sheep farms of about 820 ha. Of this area, 40 ha are improved land, which is enclosed as fields by stone dykes; about half of this is cultivated in a rotation of fodder crops, followed by three or four years of grass. The purpose of these crops is to supply winter feeding for a sheep stock of some 1,200 ewes, mainly of Border Cheviot or Black Face breeds, worked by a shepherd and his dogs. There are often herds of twenty-five to thirty-five hill cattle, which are cross bred Blue-Greys; in the uplands of the south-west, Galloway cattle are popular. The suckled calves are sold at local auction markets in October, and the lambs in August and September.

The problem for the hill-farmer is that of efficient grass management and utilization. He has to contend with a growing season of 190 days on the hill, but has to provide feeding for his animals for 365 days, using basic supplies of fodder from the arable land, and some purchased feeding stuffs. The livestock is outwintered. There is a trend towards fencing areas of the hillsides as grazing units to obtain maximum summer pasturage, while retaining sufficient roughage for the winter; this is labour saving, as it reduces costs of shepherding.

The social and economic problem of depopulation in the hill regions and remote areas is shared by the Highlands and the Uplands. Both suffer from soil erosion—centuries of moor-burning and over-grazing have broken the peat moss and grass and heather.

The wayfarer may walk where he will in the Uplands if he uses care and shows consideration: odious only are the litter louts, the dyke breakers and the casual incendiaries, or those who cannot keep their dogs under strict control or cannot bother to shut gates. The region abounds in drove roads and secluded rights of way for the walker.

# DAIRY FARMING; Dunbartonshire

Linear swells and hollows in alignment with the most recent ice movements are common features in the Lowlands. These swells or 'drumlins' are composed either of glacial debris or of rock, but frequently they are an amalgam of debris and rock (*foreground*). There are spreads of these hump-backed drumlins in and around Glasgow, which is a city of hills. The hummocks are interspersed with marshy ground, and the soils tend to be intractable wet clays, conducive to the growing of grass and stock rearing rather than to arable cropping.

A dominant agricultural enterprise in the west Lowlands is thus the dairy farm. Ayrshire is renowned for its herds of brown and white cows, grazing out of doors from May to October. There is very little snow but winter time brings frosts when grass will not grow, and herds must be fed in the byre and the cattle court. Scavenger flocks of sheep from the uplands are wintered on the grazing, and the farmer may have profitable sidelines such as intensive poultry and pig production.

All the Scottish dairy herds are tuberculin tested, and the milk is collected and distributed through the Scottish Milk Marketing Board which supervises the industry. The typical farm house and steading are built round a courtyard open on one side; there are refrigerated milk tanks in the dairies, and tanker lorries collect the milk daily from the farms. The average size of a dairy herd is fifty to seventy milk cows, whereas 70 per cent of the European farmers in the Common Market have only one dairy cow each; in 1970 the average annual milk yield per dairy cow in Scotland stood at over 3,700 litres. There have been big advances in intensive grassland management and the efficient production of hay and silage. Dairy farming is no 'nine to five' job; these family farms are progressive and productive.

This view shows dairy farms set in rolling drumlin country in Dunbartonshire, with Bardowie Castle to the north of the loch (*right centre*). In the background, the Campsie Fells, consisting of igneous rock, form an extensive lava plateau with bleak, peaty surfaces and angular scarps. The Highlands, with Ben Lomond on the horizon, are visible through the Strathblane gap. The growth of the Clydeside conurbation is eating into the 'green belt' country around its perimeter. Over 1,600 hectares of Scotland's limited amount of arable land or pasture are lost to farming each year: sprawling suburbs of houses and gardens have spread across the drumlins and threaten to engulf the open countryside in asphalt and concrete.

# ARABLE FARMING; East Lothian

Crop growing and stock farming typify the east coast plains of Scotland from the Merse and the Lothians to Ross and Cromarty. Of Scotland's 6·77 million ha of agricultural land 1·1 million ha is in grass, and over 400,000 ha is in cereal cultivation; in 1970 there were 47,000 ha of potatoes and 79,000 ha of fodder crops, the rest was rough grazing.

The most rewarding soils are associated with the occurrence of sandstone as in the Lothians and Strathmore, where arable farming and stock husbandry reach their fullest development. The production of crops is directed towards supplying livestock with fodder for winter keep, and for fattening. Farm size varies from 120 to 200 ha, and the majority of the holdings are owner occupied.

Abundance, even in these favoured regions, is only won by hard effort. Although no definite crop rotation may be followed, well regulated manuring is essential to maintain fertility. Barley is the dominant cereal crop, producing yields of high quality, which may be used for seed, or for animal feeding stuffs, or sold to distilleries and breweries for malting. Potatoes, with yields of (4·8 t per ha) are a

valuable cash crop, being marketed either as seed or as 'ware', which is sold for culinary purposes. The Scottish output was worth £14 million in 1968. Scotland produces nearly 70 per cent of the British acreage of certified seed potatoes, there are 5,000 certified growers, whose potatoes are exported all over the world. The cool Scottish climate helps to prevent potato diseases.

These east coast plains are also renowned for their pedigree livestock—in particular for their herds of Aberdeen-Angus and Shorthorn cattle, the best of which

fetch high prices at the Perth sales. But there are many more commercial or store cattle, which graze on the rich pastures, and are sold as prime Scotch beef. The wintering and fattening of sheep is also common. The Scots have a surplus of livestock products.

Farm amalgamations and increasing field size are transforming the rural landscape. Scotland's arable areas have not reached the treeless and monotonous state of the 'new prairies' of southern England, but factory-like farm buildings for intensive stock rearing and storage are ubiquitous, and are replacing traditional stone-built steadings. These arable and stock farms are highly mechanized—a farm of 200 ha may have six tractors or more, plus a large selection of other machinery. The weather waits for no farmer and the equipment must be on hand when necessary. Farms of this size represent an investment of £250,000 in land, animals, crops, machinery and building.

The drift from the land has been so considerable that only 4 per cent of Scotland's labour force is engaged in agriculture. Whether a farm pays or not depends not only on weather, freedom from disease in plants and animals, good men and sound management, but also on government economic policy. Barley with a guaranteed price to the farmer is currently one of the best crops to grow. These farms have to be run as a business and their enterprises have to change as prices for their products alter and hence variations in agricultural policy can transform the face of the countryside in Britain.

# ST. ABBS; Berwickshire

St. Abbs is a small resort and fishing village on the Berwickshire coast. Its modest harbour is ringed by fishermen's houses, and protected by red sandstone cliffs which rise to over 92 m. The coast is rugged and inhospitable with few beaches but an abundance of smugglers' coves. St. Abb's Head, with its lighthouse, is an imposing and welcoming landmark to the north.

St. Abbs has only a few fishing boats, but Eyemouth to the south maintains a fleet of sixty boats and crabs and lobsters are fished from near-by Burnmouth. Scotland's east coast is studded with fishing ports of varying size and significance from here to the Moray Firth and Caithness; the west coast has a similar abundance from Ballantrae to Kinlochbervie.

60

There are about 500 Scottish seine net boats of up to 15 m in length, fishing the Minch, the Firth of Clyde and the North Sea. East coast craft, wooden built and smartly painted with varnished wheelhouses, are often seen in the western harbours—their registration marks give them away—INS for Inverness, PD for Peterhead, BF for Banff and FH for Fraserburgh. They fish the Minch between the mainland and the Outer Hebrides for white fish, such as haddock, sole and whiting, and for herring, according to the season. The diversity of catches in the inshore fisheries is however considerable.

Expanding ports such as Lochinver and Kinlochbervie in Sutherland have no rail head and rely upon road transport over winding but improved routes to convey their landings to market. New harbour facilities and ice-making plants have been constructed and the fishermen's cars at the pierhead are evidence of their hard work and growing prosperity.

Renewed attention is being given to west coast fisheries in the Hebrides where fleets, fostered by government aid, are being rewarded with worthwhile landings of white fish and crustaceans. Experiments with fish farming of sole and plaice are proceeding at Ardtoe in Mull. On the western seaboard holidaymakers seeking tough and active pursuits are turning to sea angling, a sport for which its sea-lochs and islands are particularly well suited.

# WESTFIELD; Fife

Scattered through the coalfields of Lanarkshire, Ayrshire, the Lothians and Fife are clusters of coal bings, monuments to an industry once characterized by numerous small collieries. The Westfield opencast coal-mine can be seen as the reverse of a waste tip: an enormous hole from which coal is excavated and transported to the surface along winding road by mammoth trucks.

The principle upon which opencast mining is based is that the soil, and overburden, which cover the coal seams near to the surface can be stripped away by large grabs. The spoil is preserved, so that when the seams have been fully exploited, it can be replaced and the surface can revert to agricultural or other uses.

Here at Kinglassie work began in 1952 and millions of tonnes of spoil have been removed. The coal is loaded by the grabs, three of which can be seen in the photograph, on to dump trucks with a load capacity of 65 tonnes. At the surface the coal is unloaded on to conveyor belts for transportation to railway sidings, whence it is carried to the thermal power station at Cockenzie on the Firth of Forth and to the Lurgi gas-producing unit at Westfield.

There are several advantages in opencast mining over the more conventional shaft mining. It gives easier access to thick seams; it saves investment in expensive lifting gear, underground lighting, ventilation and transport and it allows the efficient use of large machines. Beyond this, the possibility of returning landscape to a natural appearance after an extractive industry has served its purpose is an enormous social and economic advantage for a highly populous nation with a limited extent of useful surface area.

62

# BILSTON GLEN; Midlothian

The modern design of the pithead buildings and lifting gear shown in this view of Bilston Glen colliery in Midlothian should not conceal the fact that coal-mining is a declining industry in Scotland. The record of Rothes colliery (see page 123) is a grim reminder of the effects of rapid economic change on even new mining projects.

In 1947, when the British coal industry was nationalized, Scottish pits, on the four major coalfields, produced 24 million tonnes a year; by 1972 the figure had been reduced to 11·8 million tonnes. Many accessible coal seams were exhausted. In other collieries the complications in mining as a result of faulted strata, fractured seams and the intrusion of igneous rocks in the sedimentary rock beds in which coal occurs, contributed to the decline in annual production. Many collieries have closed and thousands of miners have been made redundant. On the other hand some new 'long-life' collieries have been opened, using intensive mechanization to achieve a high level of productivity per man shift.

About 2,000 men are employed at Bilston Glen and they produce a million tonnes of coal a year—giving a high productivity of 2·7 tonnes per man shift. The coal is used in thermal power stations. The role of coal as a fuel for electricity production is a controversial issue. There is a strong case for using oil in place of coal, while the potential of nuclear power stations has already been demonstrated. The loss of overseas markets, the substitution of alternative fuels for domestic heating, the change from steam to diesel on the railways, and the introduction of oil into industries previously dependent on coal are irreversible trends not confined to Scotland, but common to all industrially advanced countries. While there is cause to welcome the decline of an industry which took a heavy toll on life and landscape, there is a feeling of regret for those communities which developed a distinctive culture focused on the pit, and which are currently suffering social and economic dislocation.

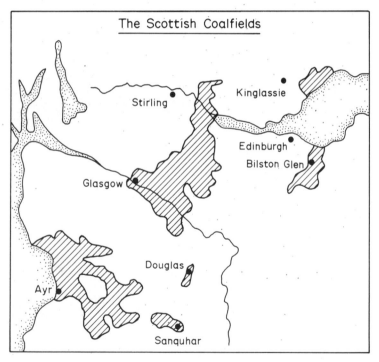

The Scottish Coalfields

Stirling

Kinglassie

Edinburgh

Bilston Glen

Glasgow

Douglas

Ayr

Sanquhar

# LONGANNET; Fife

Longannet power station is situated on the north bank of the Forth estuary facing Grangemouth docks (see page 70). It is the largest thermal power station in Europe and its potency can be expressed in these terms: in every three hours it produces more power than the muscle energy of the entire working population of Britain!

In this photograph the power station can be seen (*left centre*) standing on the level river bank. To the right of the Kincardine Bridge, upstream from Longannet, is the Kincardine power station. Ash from this power station was pumped to the area where Longannet now stands to provide a base for construction. Longannet is located, therefore, on partially reclaimed land. The massive lagoons in the foreground will eventually be filled with pulverised fuel ash from Longannet.

The plant has cost over £100 million and contains four 600,000 kW (2·16 million MJ) steam turbine generating sets. The power is produced with coal from near-by collieries. Although Scottish coal is relatively expensive special pricing arrangements have been made between the National Coal Board and the South of Scotland Electricity Board. Thus Longannet is now helping to maintain 10,000 Scottish miners in work. The coal is delivered by road, rail and a 11 km underground tunnel at the rate of 10,000 tonnes per day.

Longannet is well-sited in terms of availability of coal, and water for cooling purposes. It is also reasonably placed in terms of present-day electricity consumption in central Scotland. The provision of expensive transmission lines from the power station to the consumer is an important factor in the power industry. On the other hand electricity does offer industrial consumers flexibility in the location of their plant. The attraction of abundant power supplies to those industries which consume large amounts of electricity relative to other resources should assist the economic expansion of the Forth estuary.

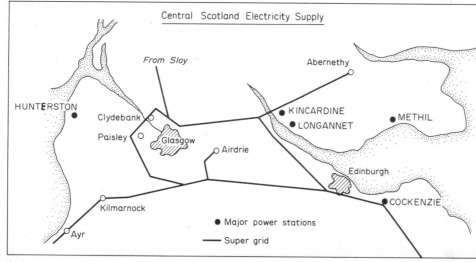

Central Scotland Electricity Supply

# LOCH LONG; Argyllshire

A giant tanker moored alongside a jetty in a beautiful Scottish loch seems incongruous, especially as the oil storage tanks set in the rocky hollows on the loch side are so few and so small. The depth of the water, the shelter afforded by the mountains bounding the loch, the lack of tidal interference for docking and the shortage of suitable deep-water harbours in Britain for the enormous modern tankers are the keys to the puzzle. For the Finnart oil terminal, situated on Loch Long in Argyllshire, is linked by subterranean pipeline to the BP oil refinery at Grangemouth (see page 70). The 17 m depth of water at the jetty heads allows tankers of up to 300,000 tonnes capacity to berth at Finnart.

The two jetties at Finnart handle oil mainly from the Middle East. The first jetty came into operation in 1951 and the second was completed in 1959. The oil is discharged at impressive speed: 6,000 tonnes of crude oil per hour can be pumped via storage tanks into the pipeline.

Finnart is the only tanker terminal in Britain capable of berthing such large vessels fully laden. Tankers call to discharge part of their cargoes before sailing to other European ports. The oil pipeline from the Forties' Field will also bring oil to the Firth of Forth and a tanker terminal is to be constructed there.

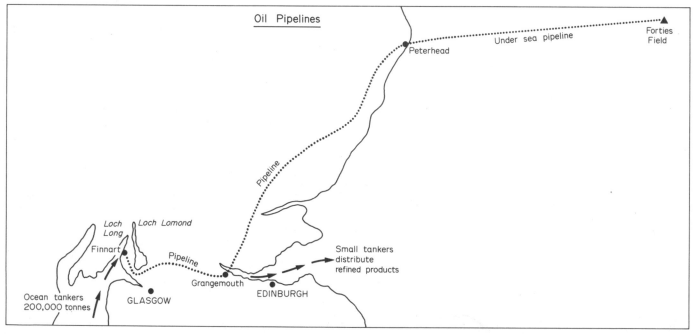

Oil Pipelines

68

# GRANGEMOUTH; Stirlingshire

Grangemouth is an industrial boom town. Its dynamic growth is due entirely to the oil-refining industry which started here in 1924. Crude oil was delivered to the refinery in 12,000 tonne tankers which could easily enter the port's dock gates. Petrol and kerosene were the major products and total annual production averaged 360,000 tonnes in the 1930s. The annual production of the refinery is seven million tonnes. There are a wide range of products including butane and propane (liquefied gas), tractor vaporizing oil, kerosene, sulphur for sulphuric acid and explosives, tetramer for chemicals, motor gasoline, benzene and naphtha.

The shallowness of the estuary, the docks, with their lock gates, built out to the deep-water channel, and the extent of the BP oil complex on the former estuarine mud flats all stand out clearly in the photograph. Directly

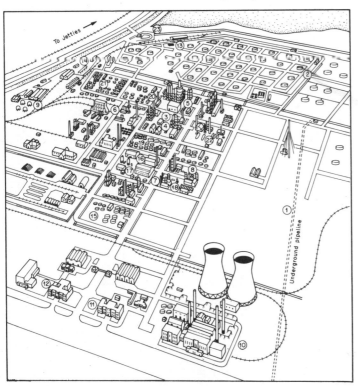

| | |
|---|---|
| 1 Finnart pipeline | 14 White oil road and rail despatch |
| 2 Crude and finished products tankage | 15 Intermediate tankage |
| 3 Crude oil distillation unit | 16 Bauxite plant |
| 4 Vacuum distillation unit | 17 Acid and soda treatment plant |
| 5 Catalytic cracking plant | 18 Copper chloride treatment plant |
| 6 Sulphur production plant | 19 Intermediate tankage |
| 7 SO$_2$ plant | 20 Heavy oil blending oil |
| 8 Solutizer plant | 21 Spirit blending area |
| 9 Propane and butane storage and despatch | 22 Crude oil distillation unit |
| 10 Steam boiler and power station | 23 Fuel oil road despatch |
| 11 Laboratory | |
| 12 Administration building | |
| 13 Fuel oil rail despatch | |

associated with the refinery and linked by pipelines to it, are many major petrochemical installations including British Hydrocarbon Chemicals, Forth Chemicals, Grange Chemicals, Bakelite-Xylanite and ICI Dyestuffs Division.

The production of plastics, synthetic materials and a variety of chemical products is carried on in these satellite plants. The export of many of the finished products has resulted in an expansion programme for Grangemouth docks which includes a new container terminal. The oil is imported via the Finnart pipeline (see page 68) but timber, iron ore, wood-pulp and foodstuffs also come into the docks. In addition to petro-chemicals, the exports include tractors, carpets, whisky and steel. Grangemouth's position makes it one of Scotland's leading gateways to the European Common Market.

# CRUACHAN; Argyllshire

Travelling west from Glasgow to Oban one passes through the Pass of Brander, a striking glacial trough formed along the shatter belt related to a mesh of fault lines. The southern slopes of this narrow gorge rise steeply from the pitch-black waters of the narrowest part of Loch Awe. The Pass was the scene of an ambush on Robert Bruce in 1308 and today it is followed by the main road and railway to Loch Etive and Oban.

To the north the slopes rise from the Loch to the peak of Ben Cruachan (1,125 m). The dam set in the saddle and the power lines suggest electricity generation, but they give no hint of the fact that beneath Cruachan's slopes a cavern, large enough to accommodate Glasgow Cathedral, has been excavated, and by a major feat of engineering a power station capable of producing 300,000 kilowatts (1·08 million MJ) has been installed. Technically, this is a pumped storage scheme: electricity is produced for peak-time consumption in Glasgow and Clydeside; during off-peak periods electricity from a Clydeside thermal power station pumps water from Loch Awe up to the reservoir behind the dam. The operating head of water is 366 m. Loch Awe itself is contained by a smaller dam (*left centre*).

Cruachan was opened by the Queen in October 1965. The project indicates the usefulness of the Highlands as a limited source of water power and the possibility of constructing massive engineering schemes without serious loss to the impressive mountain scenery. Conducted tours of the underground caverns are an added tourist attraction in this area.

# HUNTERSTON; Ayrshire

The output of the South of Scotland Electricity Board's nuclear power station at Hunterston together with the power from the Atomic Energy Authority's Chapelcross works on the Solway has made Scotland the nation with the highest *per capita* nuclear power production in the world.

Hunterston was opened in 1964. Situated on the Ayrshire coast, its site was determined by the availability of water for cooling purposes, the flatness of the land with rock suitable for foundations, and the distance from large urban centres. This safety element which was so important in determining the location of the first wave of Britain's nuclear power stations is now of much less significance.

In contrast to conventional power stations Hunterston does not need rail transport for bulky fuels or space for the disposal of ash or the storage of coal. There is no problem of smoky chimneys or air pollution. The buildings, occupying some 65 hectares are described by the South of Scotland Electricity Board as blending with 'their magnificent surroundings like a sundial in a country garden'. In the buildings are two graphite reactors set in protective concrete shielding. Within the reactors are uranium fuel elements—bars of uranium 588 cm long and 2·54 cm in diameter—which are fed into the 3,000 channels running through the graphite blocks. Carbon dioxide gas is blown through the channels and becomes intensely hot through contact with the heat produced from a nuclear chain reaction in the uranium. The heat is transferred from the gas to water in steam raising units, and the steam drives turbo generators which produce electricity in the conventional manner.

The availability of electricity, the suitability of the neighbouring land for industrial building, and the abundance of water supplies have proved attractive for industrialists wishing to establish large industrial installations close to Clydeside. Included in the list of potential developments are oil refineries, and associated petrochemical plants, an iron-ore terminus and an integrated steel mill. Strong local pressures seek to limit, or even exclude, such industries. Their main argument is that the local natural beauty will attract tourists and, if suitable amenities are provided for them, these would prove to be more profitable than large-scale industry. Alternative industrial locations of lower amenity value, either inland or on reclaimed areas, have been suggested in order to achieve economic growth without loss of environment.

# THE BIG MILL; Ravenscraig, Motherwell, Lanarkshire

The iron industry was in the van of the economic expansion of Lanarkshire in the eighteenth and nineteenth centuries. Capital, generated by Glasgow's successful trading activities, was available to pay for the exploitation of local resources of coking coal, 'black-band' ironstone, and limestone (used in the smelting process). When the local ironstone was exhausted iron ore was imported. In the nineteenth century first the Bessemer process and then the Gilchrist Thomas process led to steel becoming relatively more important, especially in ship-building and engineering. By the late nineteenth century the iron and steel industry was scattered through Lanarkshire, the most important centres being Motherwell, Coatbridge, Airdrie and Bellshill.

In the twentieth century rationalization has led to a concentration of the industry in a few centres. Motherwell is one such and here is the 'big mill', opened in 1962 for the manufacture of strip sheet steel. The steel is produced by a continuous rolling process and the works has a capacity for producing over one million tonnes of steel a year, 33 per cent of Scotland's steel production of 3·3 million tonnes. The location of this enormous installation was largely determined by the central government's policy of revitalizing areas, such as parts of central Scotland, which were suffering from economic decline. An efficient steel industry is a prerequisite for many other growth industries. Thus the big mill is directly associated with the car factory at Linwood (see page 116).

Apart from the availability of labour and the traditions of metallurgy in the area, Ravenscraig would seem to be a poor site for the big mill. Iron ore has to be imported via the General Terminus Quay in Glasgow which can take ore carriers up to only 28,000 tonnes; the Lanarkshire collieries have been closed and coking coal is now imported from the north of England; while limestone is now brought in from the Pennines. There are plans for the modernization of the steel industry in Scotland and for the expansion of the steel strip mill.

# BATHGATE; West Lothian

The red ochre bings scattered through West Lothian are an ugly reminder that this was the birthplace of Britain's oil industry. The oil was extracted from the shales which now form the bings and was refined at Pumpherston. As recently as 1962 the refinery was still functioning. The bings are now blots on the landscape, though the material is being removed for brick manufacture and road building.

The origin of the shale oil industry is associated with James 'Paraffin' Young. This Glaswegian, born in 1796, developed an interest in chemistry while working at John Anderson's Trade and Technical College. In 1850, after successful experiments with oil from Derbyshire, he patented a process for removing oil from coal. Boghead cannel, or parrot coal, derived from seams around Bathgate in West Lothian, was found to be exceptionally oil productive. The refinery built at Bathgate was the first oil refinery in the world. Paraffin oil and candle wax were the end products. The exhaustion of the Boghead coal seams led to experiments using the local Carboniferous shales. A tonne of the richer shales was found to produce 360 litres of oil. Ammonia was an even more important product of the oil than either paraffin or candle wax, for this, when combined with sulphuric acid, produced ammonium sulphate, a valuable agricultural fertilizer. Production of oil fell from an annual 11,000 tonnes in the 1930s until the closure of the refinery in 1962. However, with the massive petro-chemical complex focused on Grangemouth, the importance of this part of Scotland in the world oil industry has been maintained.

# NEWHOUSE INDUSTRIAL ESTATE; Lanarkshire

The electronics industry is at the heart of Scotland's technological revolution. The sequence of man-power, horse-power, water-power, steam-power and electric-power must now be extended to mechanical-brain power and Scotland is a world leader in this sophisticated development.

In 1959 there were 7,400 employees in the Scottish electronics industry; by 1974 the figure had exceeded 20,000 and Scotland ranked alongside the U.S.A., Japan, Germany and England as a world supplier of data processing and retrieval systems and in the manufacture of micro-circuits.

American firms dominate the Scottish electronics industry but there are a number of important British companies as well. They are to be found throughout the central Lowlands, especially in Fife and Edinburgh in the east, and Lanarkshire and Clydeside in the west. IBM (Greenock), National Cash Register (Dundee), Burroughs (Cumbernauld), Ferranti (Edinburgh), Elliott Automation (Glenrothes) and AEI (Glenrothes and Kirkcaldy) are among the leading firms with factories in Scotland.

The Honeywell Controls factory is located alongside the Glasgow–Edinburgh motorway at Newhouse. The firm is one of the early American 'invaders'. In 1948 it opened its first plant with sixty employees. It now employs 5,000 employees in five factories.

Another major occupant of the industrial estate is General Motors (Scotland) which produces earth moving equipment (*upper centre*). The plant employs over 2,000 people. The production includes scrapers, front-end loaders, crawler tractors and dumper trucks. Over 70 per cent of the units are exported and the plant helps to make Scotland second only to the U.S.A. as a producer of earth moving equipment.

The success of these industries is the result of several factors. The most important is the encouragement given by central and local government to American businessmen seeking access to a European market. Advance factories; a pool of skilled labour; improving communications by road, rail, air and sea; developing educational facilities for the training of skilled workers; and the development of complete new towns are some of the features which attract industrial investment. That success breeds success is evident to any observer of this aspect of the Scottish industrial scene.

# SELKIRK; Selkirkshire

Woollen mills clustered on a valley floor; stone-built houses scattered on the valley side; a neat rugby pitch on a well-drained central site: these are features which are typical of the border mill town. Selkirk shares them with such towns as Galashiels, Hawick and Jedburgh.

The woollen towns occupy an area relatively remote from the urban centres of the central Lowlands. Their focus is in the Tweed valley which provided the water for washing the fleeces from upland flocks and later gave an early form of power to drive the wheels at the original mills. Similar conditions were found in the late eighteenth and early nineteenth centuries in such areas as the West Riding, mid-Wales and Gloucestershire. Later improved technology, coupled with the introduction of high quality imported fleeces, led to a rationalization of the woollen industry and a relocation of the mills.

In the mid-nineteenth century Selkirk was renowned as a shoe producing town (the townsfolk were known as 'souters' or shoe makers); by 1870 the mill owners were moving their woollen mills from Galashiels and other such places to Selkirk, where the flat valley floor of the Ettrick Water offered suitable sites for the construction of larger mills. These mills can be seen in the left foreground. The regularity of their layout contrasts with the profusion of buildings on the hillside. As befits an ancient burgh the town hall and market place are the focus of the community. Proudly remembering the years 1799–1832 when Sir Walter Scott was Sheriff of Selkirk, the town looks back to even more distant times when it annually celebrates the Common Riding of the Marches.

In the town's mills are now produced many varieties of woollen textiles including 'reproduction tartans', tweed, cashmere and mohair goods, fine lambswool and Shetland wool for the knitting trade, yarn for carpets and blankets, cloths for men's suiting and overcoats, and piece goods for ladies' fashion clothing.

Although in a relatively isolated position, the border towns have shown that they can remain leaders in a wide range of textiles by producing high quality goods. Based on this prosperity the towns have established their own local cultures, perhaps shown most vigorously in the prowess of the local rugby teams and in the Riding of the Marches.

# LAGAVULIN; an Islay Distillery, Argyllshire

Lagavulin was once the site of smuggling bothies, which had all the essentials for distillation—pure water, barley and peat—close at hand. The Scotch whisky industry has its origins in antiquity, but only some 20 per cent of the units in production today date back beyond 1823, when a new Excise Act, and strict control of illicit distilling, gave impetus to a commercial industry. Smugglers themselves took out licences at that time.

Malt or pot still whisky is made from malted barley, the wash being double distilled in copper pot stills of traditional pattern, although wood or coal firing has been replaced by steam heating from oil fired boilers. The malt is dried over peat fires in pagoda shaped kilns—this imparts the unique flavour to Scotch whisky.

In the mid-nineteenth century, the Coffey or Patent Still, yielding alcohol by continuous distillation, was introduced to Lowland Scotland; its product is described as patent still or grain whisky, being derived from maize and barley.

Whisky blending developed after this innovation; malt and grain whiskies are selected to give a consistent and recognizable blend, of which more than 100 brands are well known the world over. Blends are for those whose taste prefers a lighter whisky, but there are also pure malt whiskies for the connoisseur.

The industry has greatly expanded in recent years: over 120 distilleries are in active production, eight of them in Islay. The annual output is in excess of 681 million proof litres a year, while no less than 1,773 million proof litres are maturing in warehouses in Scotland. Scotch whisky must be stored in cask for at least three years before it is fit to drink. Firms have turned increasingly to overseas markets with 340 million litres going abroad each year. Scotch whisky has become the leading export of Scotland. Consumption in Britain barely exceeds 45 millions, as duty stands at over £4·40 per proof litre.

The licensees of Lagavulin are White Horse Distillers Ltd., a subsidiary of the Distillers' Company Ltd. An island location brings transport problems: D.C.L.'s Islay distilleries are served by their own 'puffer', *The Pibroch*. Effluent is run to waste in the sea—this tell-tale sign turns the water milky, and was at one time the evidence of illicit distilling which gave the smugglers away to the excisemen.

Similar pollution in rivers has serious consequences, which distillers and others are forced to arrest by installing disposal plants.

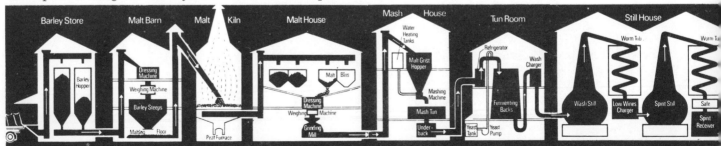

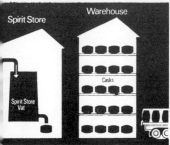

Spirit Store

Warehouse

Spirit Store Vat

Casks

# THE PULP MILL; Corpach, Inverness-shire

Pulp and paper; hydro-electric power; aluminium production—these are typical products of a developing Scandinavian fjord community. In this view across Loch Eil and Loch Linnhe can be seen a Scottish community with these same characteristics.

Beneath the massive bulk of Ben Nevis (*right*) lies Fort William. Following the east shore of Loch Linnhe, one reaches the estuary of the river Lochy. Here (*upper centre*) pipes carrying water for the hydro-electric power for the British Aluminium Company smelter at Lochaber can be seen as two parallel lines on the mountain slope. The pipes mark the end of a 24 km tunnel from the dam at Loch Treig. At Lochaber alumina brought by rail from Burntisland in Fife is smelted into aluminium ingots, which are then sent on to Falkirk for further processing.

Continuing along the sweep of the bank, one can see the harbour at Corpach at the western end of the Caledonian Canal. Here small vessels carrying timber from Scandinavia discharge their cargo for the Wiggins Teape paper mill, the factory which dominates the foreground. Opened in 1966, the mill has a labour force of nearly 1,000 and produces high quality paper by chemical processing. Timber is brought from various parts of the Highlands as well as Scandinavia. The West Highland Railway, once threatened with complete closure, has been partially saved, for along the line from Crianlarich in Perthshire two special timber trains travel daily to the mill.

The success of the smelter and the mill have been an encouragement to the Highlands and Islands Development Board to attract other large scale industries to the north of Scotland. If rural depopulation and the drift of young people from the Highlands southwards is to be checked, such new industry is essential.

# INVERGORDON; Ross and Cromarty

Until the 1960s Invergordon was best known for its naval functions but the naval base closed in 1956 and since then there has been an intensive campaign to attract other forms of employment to this part of the Cromarty Firth.

Today Invergordon is the hub of a relatively new regional phenomenon—MIDAS, marine industrial development areas. Large scale modern industry, dependent on imported raw materials, needs port facilities capable of handling ships exceeding 500,000 tonnes. Storage facilities, factories, transport systems and the associated urban growth all require extensive level land. Invergordon's potential for such expansion, notably in aluminium production and petro-chemical industries, was recognized by the Highlands and Islands Development Board and by individual industrialists. The photograph opposite shows the layout of the British Aluminium Company smelter and on this page we see the smelter in its completed state. More than a thousand men were employed in its construction and now the workforce is approximately 600. In the recent photograph can be seen the new jetty and the overhead conveyor to the two large storage silos. The alumina is reduced in the four long buildings in the foreground. Production started here in 1971 and the full capacity of the plant is 100,000 tonnes annually.

In the future it is anticipated that petro-chemical industries will be located here, associated with North Sea oil exploitation. Invergordon, a small coastal village in 1961 with a population of 1,640, will be transformed into an urban community.

# COMMUNICATIONS; Dunbartonshire

The long history of occupancy and land use in central Scotland is revealed in this picture. To the right of the factory chimneys in the centre, one can trace the line of the Antonine Wall. This earth bank marked out by Julius Agricola in A.D. 80, and paralleled by a roadway, runs from Carriden on the Firth of Forth to Old Kilpatrick on the Clyde. Here it fringes the perimeter of Cumbernauld new town (*top right*). West of the railway viaduct (*left centre*) the site of a Roman fort has been covered by a railway embankment.

The general disposition of lines of communication from right to left reflects the west to east trend of routes in the narrow belt of lowland extending from Glasgow to Edinburgh and from Stirling to Perth and Dundee. Successive stages of transport history are portrayed by the canal, railways and dual carriageway shown here.

The Forth and Clyde Canal was opened in 1790 and the occasion was marked by the passage of the 80-tonne sailing ship *Agnes* along its length. It was closed in 1963 having failed to prove an efficient means of transport in competition with modern rail and road services. Since 1963 the canal has been allowed to decay into a state of disrepair. So far its potential for cruising, fishing and canalside walking has not been realized.

The Edinburgh–Glasgow railway line was completed in 1842. From the mid-nineteenth century onwards railways proved to be a fast, economical means of carrying goods and passengers. The Edinburgh–Glasgow route is still the busiest in Scotland; the inter-city diesel trains provide frequent passenger services, which could be further improved if electrification schemes are accepted.

In this century the primacy of the railways has been challenged by road transport. Dramatic changes in road building techniques and in the number and type of vehicles have revolutionized land transport, and in many areas brought about rail closures. Running parallel, diagonally across the photograph, are the Glasgow to Stirling dual carriageway and a disused railway line.

Improved communications are a fundamental part of the infrastructure upon which a modern economy is based. Cumbernauld prides itself on having come to terms with the motor-car. The effects on smaller older communities such as Dennyloanhead (*bottom right*) are more difficult to control.

# THE HAMILTON BY-PASS; Lanarkshire

The Glasgow to Carlisle road carries three-quarters of all commercial traffic between Scotland and England. Since 1945 this road has been reconstructed as a dual carriageway with sections of motorway standard (M74). The photograph shows an interchange on this road on a section known as the Hamilton by-pass, which was completed on 1 December 1966.

Occupying 40 hectares the by-pass eliminates traffic congestion in the urban complex of Hamilton, Motherwell, Larkhall and Uddingston. The valley floor of the Clyde proved to be a difficult base for road construction. 4·6 million cubic metres of clay and other soil were removed. Three colliery bings and a steel works' waste-tip were also cleared. The pools of water in the top part of the photograph were not formed by river action, but are the result of a 5 m subsidence associated with coal-mining operations in the Hamilton Low Parks area. A further complication was the need to reroute the Avon, a tributary of the Clyde, before road construction could commence.

In addition to providing an advanced free-flow road system, the interchange incorporates pedestrian footpaths and cycle tracks which can be seen adjacent to the motorway. These link Hamilton and Motherwell.

In an age of fast inter-city road travel, cross-roads, traffic lights and pedestrian crossings are clearly out-dated. This elaborate system of slip-roads and flyovers keeps pedestrians and vehicles apart and gives easy access from one major road to another. However, the complex intersections require large areas of land and very substantial capital investment.

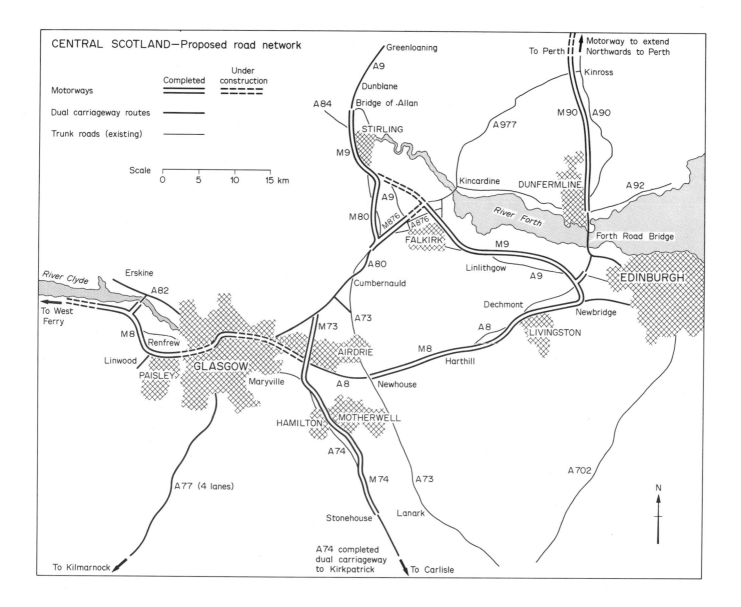

CENTRAL SCOTLAND—Proposed road network

Motorways    Completed    Under construction

Dual carriageway routes

Trunk roads (existing)

Scale   0   5   10   15 km

Greenloaning
A9
To Perth   Motorway to extend Northwards to Perth
Dunblane
Kinross
A84   Bridge of Allan
M90   A90
STIRLING
A977
M9
DUNFERMLINE
A9
Kincardine
A92
M80   M876
A876
River Forth
FALKIRK
M9
Forth Road Bridge
A80
Linlithgow   EDINBURGH
Cumbernauld
A9
River Clyde
Erskine
A82
Dechmont
Newbridge
To West Ferry
A73
A8   LIVINGSTON
M8   Renfrew
M73
Linwood
AIRDRIE
M8   Harthill
PAISLEY   GLASGOW
Maryville
A8   Newhouse
MOTHERWELL
HAMILTON
A74
A77 (4 lanes)
M74   A73
Stonehouse   Lanark
A702
To Kilmarnock
A74 completed dual carriageway to Kirkpatrick   To Carlisle
N

93

# KYLESKU; Sutherland

One of the remote and surprising places in the northern Highlands is Kylesku, where the narrows of Loch Cairnbawn, an inlet of Eddrachillis Bay, are guarded by Garbh Eilean (*right*) and several other rocky islets.

A fast car ferry sails the 200 m of water, linking Unapool about a mile away on the south side and Kylestrome on the north. It is a sheltered crossing, the Loch being hemmed in by Quinag (810 m) and Glasven (775 m) which protect the Kyle to the south. Eastwards, the waters of Lochs Glendhu and Glencoul penetrate the mountainous interior, where the waterfall of Eas-Coul-Aulin, over 180 m high, is approachable only by boat or on foot.

From Kylesku the road leads south to Lochinver and Ullapool and northwards through the Reay Forest to Scourie and Durness. Bridges are considered too expensive and traffic too light throughout the year to justify their construction at such a point. Certainly ferry crossings in Scottish lochs could be improved by more drive-on, drive-off craft, in the running of which there are lessons to be learned from Norwegian practice. Although the queues may be lengthy in summer the ferry at Kylesku, which is operated by Sutherland County Council, is free. At the other ferries—Strome, Ballachulish, Corran and Kyle of Lochalsh, travellers have to wait and pay too.

Tourists have little or no alternative but to travel through areas such as this by road. There is an unrealized potential for cruise liners of moderate size to explore the western coastline, but there are no regular passenger cruises to the sea-lochs of the Scottish mainland and its fringing islands.

# THE FORTH BRIDGES;
# Fife and West Lothian

The construction of the Tay (see page 105) and Forth road bridges has brought improved communications to Fife, and a faster road from the Borders to Aberdeen and the north-east. However Fifers complain that the road tolls on the bridges make Fife the only county in Britain which you pay to enter and leave.

The original Forth Bridge is seen in the lower half of the photograph. It was built between 1882 and 1890 and carries two railway tracks over a distance of more than 2·4 km. The steel structure has a cantilever design, with three main piers from which six cantilever arms rise and project. The main compression members of the cantilevers consist of steel tubes up to 3·7 m in diameter.

The new road bridge, for all its structural modernity, cannot overshadow the old bridge. Each has its own functional beauty. The road bridge was opened in 1964. Before this road travellers had to wait for the ferry at Queensferry or journey upstream to the Kincardine Bridge. The railway bridge is composed of 51,000 tonnes of steel, while the road bridge required 39,000 tonnes of steel and 11,300 m³ of concrete.

The bridging of the estuaries of the Tay and the Forth has greatly improved the flow of road transport along the east coast and the success of these ventures has led to a demand for similar improvements in the north-west. There, however, the terrain is more rugged and the population much less numerous.

# PRESTWICK; Ayrshire

For a nation of five million people Scotland has well-developed air transport facilities. The airport at Prestwick on the Ayrshire coast differs from the other two large airports in central Scotland—Turnhouse (Edinburgh) and Abbotsinch (Glasgow)—because it specializes in international flights. The busiest route is to the United States, and the most rapidly increasing sector of the airport's business is the provision of trans-Atlantic charter flights.

The airport was opened in 1935 and reached its peak of activity during the Second World War when, as an American military air base, it was the terminus for the trans-Atlantic ferry service. The flat land of the Ayrshire plain provides a suitable site for airport construction, especially since the increasing size of jet airliners has demanded longer runways. The new jumbo jets present no landing or take-off problems for Prestwick.

Physical features, however, are not the only considerations in airport location and development, as the controversy over the siting of a third London airport has shown. Proximity to urban centres, city-airport transport services, the availability of hotel accommodation, the effects of the noise of the enormous aircraft, and prevailing weather conditions all have to be considered. In its favour Prestwick can claim freedom from smog which sometimes paralyses metropolitan airports. Situated as it is almost on the seashore, it is able to minimize the objectionable effects of aircraft noise. Against this it lacks an airport hotel, or a station for the direct rail link with Glasgow. The delay in the construction of a by-pass round Kilmarnock has also hindered development and despite its excellent site features, Prestwick may prove in the long run to have a poor location.

# THE CRINAN CANAL; Argyllshire

Crinan is a small village where Crinan Loch meets the Sound of Jura. The canal which starts at Ardrishaig on Loch Fyne is 14 km long, and was built between 1793 and 1801. Its purpose was to enable small ships to reach the Atlantic seaboard without having to make the long and often stormy passage round the Mull of Kintyre, more than 80 km to the south. Here the yacht basin at Crinan is sheltered from the choppy waters of the loch by protective tree-clad slopes.

Crossing verdant countryside, the canal is a 'Road to the Isles' for yachtsmen travelling to the Inner Hebrides from the Clyde. As such it is valuable for recreational purposes, but it is also utilized by puffers and fishing boats. In 1958 the British Transport Commission concluded that it was unprofitable, but more significant than the Caledonian Canal, since it was used by twice as many vessels. The depth of water was inadequate and the numbers of cargo vessels was declining; but the number of yachts going through was rising yearly. In 1962 the British Waterways Board assumed responsibility for the canal, and in 1968 it was traversed by over 2,600 small craft.

Scottish authorities have turned their backs on the recreational and amenity value of waterways—this despite the preference of Scots to take their leisure beside some form of water feature by coast, loch or river. Canals have been infilled to make motorways, which is justifiable as derelict canals tend to be zones of separation, with minimal costs of land acquisition. However the Union Canal near Edinburgh is to be saved in part. With a reduction in depth for safety, boating, canoeing, fishing, picnic areas, nature trails, pony and cycle tracks all become feasible. Old canal ports have an attraction of their own, as may be seen in European cities, where residential property, restaurants and cafés abound. The canals may have no navigational function, but the character of the area around them can be transformed for the better by their presence. In Lowland Scotland there are opportunities to transform networks of derelict canals into linear parkland.

# ABERDEEN; The Silver City

Situated between the mouths of the rivers Don and Dee, Aberdeen is a thriving multi-functional city with a population of 185,000. This photograph emphasizes the role of the north-eastern royal burgh as a fishing and commercial port, but it is also a tourist centre, a university town, an administrative focus and the trading and manufacturing hub of a large area of the north-east.

For many southerners, Aberdeen is best known as a fishing port. Its proximity to the North Sea fishing grounds, to Iceland, to the middle waters of the Faroes and to the north-west, has helped to make Aberdeen the third largest British fishing port. The Fish Wharf and Fish Market stand alongside the Albert Basin and clustered around these are buildings which specialize in fish handling and processing. Speedy transport to distant markets is essential for the white fish landed here, and this is achieved by long-distance refrigerated lorries and railway wagons. 1,700 fishermen manning 120 diesel trawlers, 5 great liners and 14 seine net vessels, as well as 6,700 shore workers are dependent on the white fishing industry in Aberdeen. The city is also the foremost market for dealing with fresh Scottish salmon. In the Victoria Dock and the Tidal Harbour vessels of up to 12,000 tonnes handle general cargoes.

Beyond the docks are the buildings of down-town Aberdeen. In the 'granite city' major buildings such as Marischal College and St. Machar's Cathedral are constructed of this rock, found in the immediate hinterland. The clean, well-defined façades of the buildings lining the main thoroughfare, Union Street, are composed of the same stone.

Scattered through the city centre and spilling into the suburbs are the administrative offices, hospitals, educational facilities and commercial buildings of the city, which serves as a centre for the whole north-east and the Highlands and Islands beyond. Although it faces problems of transport, housing and urban sprawl, Aberdeen remains for the tourist the gateway to the Highlands and Royal Deeside and, with its parks, fine buildings and golden sands, it is still a holiday resort in its own right.

Aberdeen is the Scottish centre for oil exploration in the Forties field in the North Sea.

# DUNDEE; Angus

Traditionally known for its jute, jam and journalism, Dundee, the fourth city of Scotland, now has quite different claims to fame. The image of Dundee as a sprawling, rather inaccessible city with crowded tenements dominating docksides and mills is being rapidly altered. The city is, for instance, the centre of an expanding electronics industry.

The Tay road bridge (*upper left*), completed in 1966, provides a fast route to the south, running roughly parallel with the railway. Approach roads within the city are linked in a massive development programme which includes inner and outer ring roads. Such a programme cannot be tackled in isolation, and it is integrated with the replacement of old buildings with improved housing. On the photograph it is possible to pick out cleared sites and multi-storey buildings under construction.

The new buildings are not limited to domestic purposes. The University (*lower centre*), once linked with St. Andrews, can be seen as the focus of a group of associated educational buildings.

To the left of the new bridge are the Victoria and Camperdown docks and the wharves along Tayside. Into this sheltered harbour, 16 km from the open sea, come many of the raw materials for Dundee's industries. Jute remains vital to Dundee's economy despite competition from polypropylene, a woven plastic which, like jute, is used for backing carpets. Carpets, sacking and synthetic floor coverings are important Dundee products and a sign that traditional industries can adapt to technological change and can contribute to the new prosperity as well as later arrivals such as electronics and light engineering. These new industries, with both British and American finance, are especially important on the industrial estates such as Kingsway West and Blackness.

With its improved housing, transport and educational facilities and with developing commerce and industry Dundee is established as the capital of the Tayside development area.

# EDINBURGH; The Old Town

Edinburgh is the capital city of Scotland. The crag of the Castle Rock stands defiantly in the gap between the Pentland Hills and the Firth of Forth. The steep faced volcanic crag has been scoured by ice flows, and the straggling tail on whose crest the Royal Mile is aligned, is composed of rock with a veneer of glacial debris on top.

In the distance, the outcrop of a massive whin sill shows on Salisbury Crag, while eastwards smooth plateaux of sedimentary rocks, moulded into broad swells and hollows, form the gentle countryside of the Lothians.

The site of the castle is ancient; it was probably a stronghold in Neolithic times, and it is a garrisoned fortress today. Edinburgh Castle is a 'must' for tourists. There they will see the Honours of Scotland (the Scottish crown jewels), and state apartments and learn for themselves how history was made here.

It is one mile from the Castle to the Palace of Holyrood House, via the Castle Wynd, Royal Mile and Canongate. Through this long street with its towering tenements and dark closes, the teeming pageant of Scottish history has moved. This is the Old Town with the High Kirk of St. Giles, and Parliament House (where the Court of Session sits) as its core. The Palace of Holyrood House which lies at the foot of the Royal Mile is still a royal residence, and a garden party is in progress in its grounds; guests' cars crowd the park to the east.

The Royal Mile deteriorated into a picturesque slum when the titled and wealthy deserted the Old Town for the New. The reconstruction of its tenements has transformed it; Gladstone's Land, superbly restored by the National Trust for Scotland and the Saltire Society to show what a seventeenth-century mansion in the Old Town was like before it lapsed into slumdom, is well worth visiting. Some attention to shop fronts and lettering, perhaps with the inclusion of old trade signs would give the street more coherence.

The university precinct displays its controversial multi-storey developments (*right centre*). North of the Castle Rock, Waverley Station occupies the site of a former loch (*left centre*) with the North Bridge linking the Old Town with the New beyond. Princes Street (*left*) whose private houses have been replaced by shops and department stores, is one of the famous thoroughfares of Europe, and is open to bright and sunny gardens on one side; shoppers and tourists can look up into the densely packed buildings of the Old Town and to the Castle on the rock.

# EDINBURGH; The New Town

Edinburgh has been praised as 'the Athens of the North' and chided for her greyness and smoke as 'Auld Reekie'. Both descriptions are fair. The classical New Town is the finest example of Neo-Georgian town planning in Europe; it was begun to the youthful but spacious designs of James Craig in 1770, and building continued into the early nineteenth century, when the period of high taste and design was prolonged.

The Old Town, growing in population and wealth was intolerably congested. The Nor' Loch, below the Castle where Princes Street Gardens are situated, was drained, and the North Bridge constructed across the marshland to the east. Moray McLaren describes how 'the noble, the rich and the prosperous' swarmed out of the overcrowded but companionable warren of the Old Town, and sought and found spaciousness, graciousness, cleanliness, light and air, in the New Town.

The essentially rectangular pattern of the first New Town is not monotonous. St. Andrew's Square at the eastern end, (*left centre*) and Charlotte Square at the west (*upper right*) are connected by the broad and elegant thoroughfare of George Street. Queen Street with its wide, wooded gardens, is to the north, and Princes Street, with its prospects to the Old Town and the Castle, to the south. The straight handsome streets give way to palatial crescents and circuses (*upper right*) where the Water of Leith tumbles through the western margin of the New Town. In the foreground terraces border Leith Walk, which links the city with its port, Leith.

The well-built masonry, which was once cream-coloured, is now greyed with smoke. The gracious streets giving long vistas to the sea and the hills are changing too. Commercial office blocks have invaded St. Andrew's Square; shops, hotels and offices line George Street, and there are few residences in the New Town. A proposal for a ring road was only checked by the tenacity of those who appreciate the unique value of classical Edinburgh. Traffic flow and parking surveys may suggest restricting vehicular access to the New Town, where the motor-car has to be subservient to the townscape, in order to preserve the high quality of this distinctive environment.

Edinburgh's population is close to half a million and it has its share of Victorian houses, around the Old and New Towns, with modern housing estates on the outskirts and across its boundary. The transport pressures of commuting are severe; in contrast to Glasgow, the city has no underground system and no electric trains.

As Edinburgh is the capital city of Scotland its administrative functions for government and commerce are numerous; the city has its share of industry, and is a magnet for conferences and exhibitions. The International Festival of Music, Drama and the Arts is held annually in late summer, and Edinburgh was host to the Commonwealth Games of 1970, for which new stadia were constructed.

# GLASGOW DOCKS

After flowing through the bonny countryside of Clydesdale and the grime of industrial Lanarkshire, the Clyde comes to Glasgow—'the biggest, the oldest, the most maligned and the best liked town in Scotland, especially by Glaswegians'.

Glasgow has 22 km of docks along a man-made waterway. In the eighteenth century John Golborne of Chester was engaged to deepen and straighten the river by constructing jetties to make the current scour a navigable channel, and he succeeded. The river bed consisted of alluvial and glacial deposits with mercifully few rock outcrops. The wide shallow stream interspersed with islands and channels was transformed; by 1775 a passage over 2 m deep had been cut. Dredging and improvement have continued and hence there is a popular saying that 'Glasgow made the Clyde and the Clyde made Glasgow'. The excavation of a channel helped to control floods and dry sites for industry and warehouses were formed on the banks. In time, the world's greatest concentration of shipyards developed on Clydeside and during the Second World War more ships were launched here than in all the shipyards of the United States put together. The once numerous shipbuilding companies were contracted to two groups, one on the Upper and the other on the Lower Clyde.

The view (*far right*) looks westwards over the harbour, with Prince's Dock on the south bank (*left*) and Queen's Dock on the north bank (*centre*). Ship movements are directed from a control tower on top of Meadowside Granary (*upper right*) which is the largest grain storage unit in Britain.

Ships of 28,000 tonnes can sail to within 1·2 km of the city centre to unload iron ore cargoes for central Scotland's steel industry at 1,000 tonnes per hour at General Terminus Quay (*see below*). The quayside is enmeshed in railway lines and surrounded by the tenement 'canyons' of the Kingston district; such four storey stone built housing is characteristic of nineteenth-century industrial Glasgow.

In 1966 the Clyde Navigation Trust which managed the port of Glasgow became merged in Clydeport. The Kingston Bridge built high above the river to allow access to the Broomielaw has necessitated the infilling of dock areas, and the old Finnieston vehicular ferry (*see below*) has been superseded. The world-wide phenomenon of ports shifting downstream to deeper water is affecting Glasgow; will its harbour become a back water? The revolution in engineering and dredging technology favours developments in the estuary, rather than on the river.

# GLASGOW'S HOUSING PROBLEM

About one million people live in Glasgow and most of its houses were built in the boom years of the nineteenth century. Just over half the houses in the city have basic amenities, but 10,000 are totally unfit for human habitation, a further 75,000 are incapable of being brought up to standard and 50,000 houses could be improved. Hence the magnitude of Glasgow's housing problem, and the adoption of a policy of urban renewal for the total rebuilding of twenty-nine areas containing nearly one third of its people, and affecting much of the industry and commerce of the city. In the mid-1950s there were still 700,000 people living in the 7·8 sq. km of Inner Glasgow, at a density of about 160 persons per hectare. The planners aim to reduce residential densities to around 64 persons per hectare—thus only 40 per cent of the population can be rehoused *in situ*, while 60 per cent must 'overspill' to the margins of the city, to new towns or beyond.

The desperate situation has induced desperate remedies —the multi-storey flats (of which 250 blocks have been built with more to come) have shot from 8 to 19 and then to 31 storeys, reflecting the shortage of sites within the city. Such flats involve massive underpinning in alluvial or glacial deposits close to the Clyde (*see below*) and even chemical wastes have been pressed into service as sites. The economic costs of the multi-storey blocks may be less than the social costs. Near the city boundary housing estates with populations equivalent to that of a large market town, display a paucity of urban amenities, discounting community needs and open space provision. Rent policies have also created their own injustices.

Glasgow was once 'the dear green place'—Glasgow Green, facing the new Gorbals flats across the Clyde, is one of its fifty-five parks, some of which are being encroached upon by urban motorways and expressways. Great Western Road, a tree-lined approach of sweeping

vistas, is marked for reconstruction as an expressway.

To the visitor, Glasgow seems like a dissolving sugar cube (*see above*), the gaunt fingers of concrete in the background are residential blocks. Those in the foreground are commercial ventures in the city centre. There has been no overall consideration of the scale or panorama formed by these high rise developments. In the foreground, the approaches to the Kingston Bridge on the Inner Ring Road span the Anderston area. The landmarks of Central Station (*upper right*) and George Square (*upper centre*) are almost overwhelmed in the changing urban scene.

The scale of Glasgow's housing problem is a national one: the city is 'home' to one fifth of the people of Scotland, and it merits national action. 'Rehabilitation' is now a top priority for its crumbling sandstone tenements which are ripe for improvement, and this measure has been scarcely attempted. The roof-lifting gale of January 1968 revealed how precarious is the state of the older houses in 'the finest Victorian city in Britain'.

# AYR; Ayrshire

Of all Scotland's seaside resorts Ayr is the best known. Its safe sandy beaches attract families from Scotland's industrial towns as well as from places further afield. It provides facilities for the camper and the caravanner, for holiday-makers in hotels and boarding houses, and the chalets of a holiday camp. Like other holiday resorts it has in its population a high proportion of retired people; nearness to the city of Glasgow has resulted in the expansion of new private housing for commuters. The proposed commercial and industrial expansion of the north Ayrshire coast of the Firth of Clyde may lead to an accelerated growth of Ayr's role as a dormitory town.

In the winter months Ayr is the possession of the local residents; on the weekly market days or at the race meetings it acts as a focus for farmers from the surrounding countryside. Ayrshire is renowned for its fine dairy cattle and early potatoes, agricultural products which are responses to the rich loamy soils, equable climate and proximity to a large urban market.

In summer, however, Ayr belongs to the holidaymaker. The venue for day excursions for communities all over the west of Scotland and the centre for the annual fortnight's summer holiday, especially the Glasgow Fair holiday, Ayr acts as a magnet for families who enjoy a bustling seaside resort.

As the centre of the Burns country Ayr has certain distinctive characteristics. Although the songs and verses of Robert Burns were written in the eighteenth-century Scots vernacular, they have earned the admiration of a world-wide audience. Burns was born in Alloway, a village to the south of Ayr, in 1759 and he died in Dumfries in 1796. Burns enthusiasts pilgrimage to Ayr to see the cottage where he was born, the Burns monument, the Kirk and the Auld Brig O'Doon at Alloway and the Burns statue, the Tam O'Shanter Inn and the Twa Brigs in Ayr.

# LINWOOD; Renfrewshire

Occupying over 84,000 m³, the Chrysler Ltd. (formerly Rootes) car plant is situated at Linwood, a few miles west of Paisley near Glasgow. It consists of two distinct parts divided by a dual carriageway (running from left to right diagonally). On one side of the carriageway is the car assembly plant, on the other the car body-making factory formerly owned by the Pressed Steel Company. Each week 1,500 cars move from the works. Mainly Hillman Avengers, they are transported by special car trains to Clydeside docks for export, and by road and rail to all parts of Britain.

Scotland has a long tradition of car making—long that is in relation to the short history of the motor-car. In the early decades of the century such cars as the Argyll, Albion, Arrol-Johnson, Beardmore and Galloway were produced. An impressive display of these vintage vehicles can be seen in the Museum of Transport in Glasgow.

Rootes was a newcomer to Scotland, having been encouraged to develop at Linwood in 1963 by a government under pressure to bring growth industries to an area experiencing heavy unemployment. The extensive flat site, the near-by port facilities, the availability of labour with engineering skills and the supply of high quality sheet steel from the new Ravenscraig mill (see page 76) were all factors which contributed to the present location of the plant, especially in conjunction with government financial encouragement. The factory is now part of the Chrysler organisation.

More than 5,000 men and women are employed at Linwood. The location of this vast plant distant from other car manufacturing centres was bound to prove expensive, but it has partially solved the local unemployment problem. Moreover there are other vehicle manufacturers in mid and west Scotland, including BLMC at Bathgate, West Lothian and Scotstoun, Glasgow, and the earth-moving equipment manufacturers Terex-GM Scotland and Caterpillar situated in Lanarkshire. At Kilmarnock Massey-Ferguson produce tractors and farm machinery. These firms, representing both British and American ownership, are making a major contribution to the contemporary economic resurgence of west-central Scotland and, because of the high proportion of their output which is exported, they are helping to alleviate Britain's balance of payments problems.

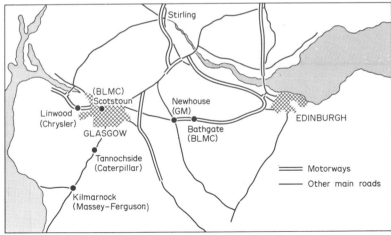

# LARGS; Ayrshire

To work in a great conurbation and to live amidst magnificent scenery is an uncommon luxury for most British commuters but one enjoyed by many residents of the north Ayrshire coastal towns. Largs on the Firth of Clyde is an example and the photograph shows its fine seascape with the islands of Great Cumbrae and, in the distance, Bute and Arran.

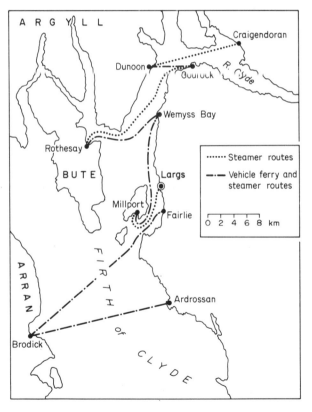

In the summer months Largs is a busy holiday town. Its safe bathing attracts visitors from Clydeside and beyond; to the yachtsman and weekend sailor it offers attractive cruising amidst the islands, on waters protected from severe weather. 'Clyde Week' in July brings yachtsmen from all over Britain. Between the two churches which dominate the Largs foreshore can be seen the pier to which come Clyde steamers on their way to Rothesay, Millport and Dunoon. Sailing 'Doon the Watter' on steamers is a traditional recreation for Glaswegians and Largs is a popular port of call.

Although its prosperity is largely based on the temporary holidaymakers and day visitors Largs is, for most of the time, a small, self-contained community. Yet it is a community which is challenged by the major changes which necessarily accompany the industrial expansion planned for the area between its southern flanks and Hunterston, some four miles to the south. At Hunterston there is a double nuclear power station (see page 74) and the flat land between there and Largs has been investigated as the site of an oil refinery and terminal, and a deep-water iron ore port, possibly with a new integrated steel works adjacent to it.

Northwards, a power station is located at Inverkip, some miles from Wemyss Bay. How long Largs can retain its suburban residential character and strong sense of community should such developments proceed is a matter for conjecture. Comprehensive planning is urgently required for this coastline, which in its variety and colour is a fitting backcloth for the magnificent estuary of the Firth of Clyde.

# CUMBERNAULD; Dunbartonshire

The attention of a world-wide television audience was drawn to Cumbernauld when it featured in a spectacular Telstar production in 1967. In the same year an international panel of town planners voted Cumbernauld the winner of the R. S. Reynolds Award for Community Architecture.

Motorists travelling from Glasgow to Stirling on the A80 pass along the base of the hill upon which Cumbernauld stands. Used for livestock grazing and small scale mining of coal and fire clay until 1954, the hill has been transformed into a town of 70,000 people.

Cumbernauld was designated a new town in 1955 and it is one of the six towns started since 1945 in central Scotland to ease the serious housing problems of the Clyde valley and other congested areas and to stimulate the expansion of new industries to revitalize a sagging economy. Four fifths of Cumbernauld's residents formerly lived in Glasgow. Industry has been attracted to its two industrial estates from elsewhere in Scotland, from England and from the United States.

The town is planned as a compact, high density housing unit, in a 'couthy' Scottish tradition, focused on the town centre of radical design which crowns the hilltop. Footpaths run down the slopes from the town centre to all the residential areas. There are no planned neighbourhoods as there are in Glenrothes (see page 122), though satellite villages are planned to house the new population which will follow from the raising of the town's target figure.

A system of roads has been designed to ensure that pedestrian and vehicle routes are completely separate. Good provision has been made for the parking and garaging of cars (the circular garages are clearly visible in the photograph). At the town centre (*top centre*) vast underground car parks are linked by stairs, escalators and lifts to a series of decks on which are located shops, offices and other commercial premises. In the residential areas there are small shopping units, schools, churches and social meeting places.

The advanced design of Cumbernauld may be a foretaste of urban living in the future.

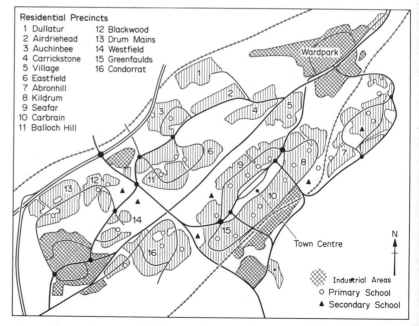

Residential Precincts
1 Dullatur
2 Airdriehead
3 Auchinbee
4 Carrickstone
5 Village
6 Eastfield
7 Abronhill
8 Kildrum
9 Seafar
10 Carbrain
11 Balloch Hill
12 Blackwood
13 Drum Mains
14 Westfield
15 Greenfaulds
16 Condorrat

Wardpark

Town Centre

N

Industrial Areas
○ Primary School
▲ Secondary School

# GLENROTHES; Fife

Glenrothes, a new town in Fife, was originally planned as a coal-mining community. It was to be associated with the new Rothes colliery, housing miners drawn to Fife from the declining coalfields of the west of Scotland. The development of the colliery began in 1946 and it was opened in 1951. However in 1962 it was closed down as uneconomic and Glenrothes lost its original economic base. Today, however, Glenrothes boasts a wide range of industrial activities, the heart of which is the largely American-owned electronics industry.

This view, taken from the west, shows very clearly the pattern of housing, schools and open spaces. The town is divided into residential precincts which surround the town centre. The photograph shows parts of the South Parks and Tanshall precincts. These precincts contain the amenities necessary for the normal day-to-day life of the residents. In the town centre (*upper left*) is a pedestrian shopping precinct incorporating a covered shopping area and large car parks. Industry is confined to specially planned sites on the periphery of the town.

The town is designed to reach a target population of 75,000. The target set in 1948 was 30,000 and this was reduced in 1956 to 18,000. Then two events radically altered Glenrothes' prospects for development. The Town Development (Scotland) Act 1957 led to an overspill agreement between Glenrothes and Glasgow, and then in the Central Scotland Plan of 1963 Glenrothes was designated a growth point. These two measures encouraged people and industry to move to the town. From this time light engineering and electronics firms found Glenrothes a promising site for development. The opening of the Forth and Tay road bridges also made the town more attractive for investment. In the light of these changes the target population was revised upwards in the belief that a prosperous planned community could be created here.

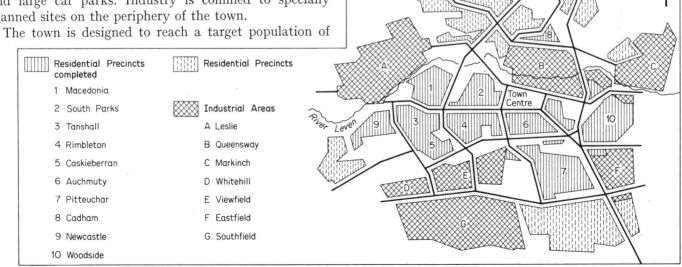

Residential Precincts completed
1 Macedonia
2 South Parks
3 Tanshall
4 Rimbleton
5 Caskieberran
6 Auchmuty
7 Pitteuchar
8 Cadham
9 Newcastle
10 Woodside

Residential Precincts

Industrial Areas
A Leslie
B Queensway
C Markinch
D Whitehill
E Viewfield
F Eastfield
G Southfield

# CULROSS; Fife

This burgh on the north shore of the Firth of Forth is a remarkably complete example of early Scottish domestic architecture. In the sixteenth century Culross, a village in size, but a royal burgh in status, participated in a prosperous trade in salt and coal with ports from the Baltic to the Netherlands. Its thriving commerce was shared with other little burghs on the Fife coast, which made the county 'a beggar's mantle fringed with gold'. When the activity declined Culross became a backwater, and was by-passed by the industrial developments of the eighteenth and nineteenth centuries. Hence its character has remained virtually unaltered.

The National Trust for Scotland has been active in promoting the restoration of the town. The Palace (*centre*), a mansion of a commercial laird, Sir George Bruce, was one of the first buildings to be saved. The Mercat Cross area (*right centre*) has been transformed by the restoring of its surrounding houses, notably the Study, the local centre of the National Trust for Scotland. Rehabilitation has extended not only to the dwelling houses, but also to the narrow cobbled causeways, which wind from the shore road to the old market place. The choir of a former Cistercian monastery is the parish church (*upper right*); Culross House overlooks the village.

To retain the individuality and charm of the burgh old houses are bought, restored to modern standards, and sold under certain safeguards; the proceeds are then used over again. The principle has been successfully applied in Anstruther, Crail, Dysart, Pittenweem and other burghs in the east Neuk of Fife, as well as at Dunkeld and Falkland. The vigorous, vernacular architecture, with stone walls 'harled' in rough cast, and roofed with red pantiles, is

an antidote to the uniformity of design which is spreading throughout Europe. Scotland was a poor country, and people were obliged to use the cheap and practical building

materials at hand. The ingenious and varied treatment of the 'little houses' commends itself to towns where older buildings should be conserved. The new town of Cumber-nauld owes something to the Scottish tradition in the simplicity and 'couthiness' of its compact neighbourhoods of closely knit homes.

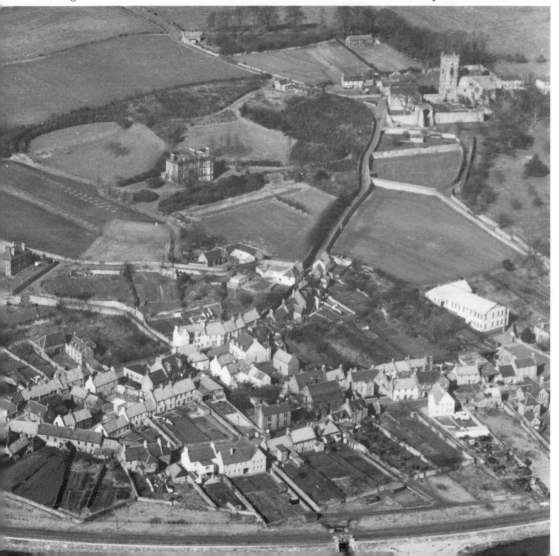

# PERTH; The Fair City

Standing on a bridging point of the river Tay and on the intersections of main roads and railway lines, Perth is an outstanding example of a town which has grown up as a route centre.

The old town of Perth (the name originated from Bertha, the Roman settlement) was situated between the Tay and the railway station. The north and south sides of this original nucleus are limited by the North and South Inches, the large parks with their riverside promenades which add so much to the amenities of the city.

The city is rich in history, but many of the old buildings, especially the ecclesiastical buildings, have been destroyed —mainly as a result of religious riots stemming from the Reformation in the sixteenth century. There is grid pattern of streets, reminiscent of central Glasgow, and despite the modern precinct around St. John's Square, it is possible to imagine 'old Perth' in the vennels, closes and back streets leading off High Street.

To the west of the railway station and extending in all directions is 'new Perth', with suburban clusters of private and council houses following the main arteries and forming crescents and avenues. Industrial buildings housing whisky blending and bottling, dyeing and glass manufacture are located near the railway yards and the small harbour on the Tay (off the photograph).

Perth is a fair city for the visitor and a base from which to explore the central Highlands. Overseas visitors include not only tourists but also cattle buyers, who come to Perth to purchase pedigree Aberdeen Angus and Shorthorn breeding stock at its famous sales.

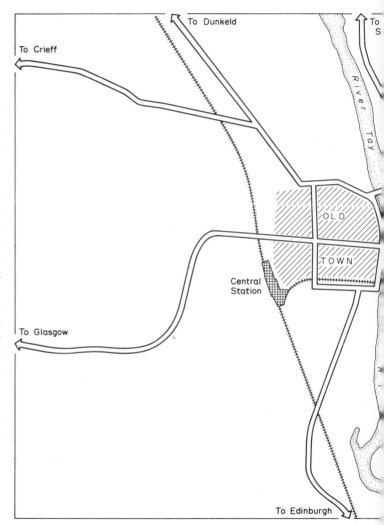

To
New
Scone

h Bridge

ueens Bridge

To Dundee

# STIRLING; Stirlingshire

Kilts and armour, dirks and axes, horses and cannon are conjured in one's mind as one stands on the battlements of Stirling castle. And for the Scot there will be memories of the stories of Robert the Bruce and William Wallace, so closely associated with the Wars of Independence. From this lofty position one can see across the modern town and beyond to the valley of the Forth. A striking landmark crowning a rocky crag is the Wallace Monument which contains a collection of armour and ancient documents.

Stirling's strategic position, dominating the Forth estuary and access from the Lowlands to the Highlands explains why so many decisive battles were fought in the area surrounding the burgh. They include Falkirk (1248), Stirling Bridge (1297), Bannockburn (1314), Sauchieburn (1488), Kilsyth (1645) and Sheriffmuir (1715). It is this dominant location which determines Stirling's present-day significance.

At the terminus of a motorail route, Stirling is the starting point for many holidaymakers from the south. At the junction of main roads to Perth and the northeast, to Falkirk, Edinburgh, and the south, to Glasgow and the south-west, and to Callander and the Trossachs, Stirling is the focus of the routes through the gap between the Campsie Fells and the Ochils.

Apart from being a tourist centre, Stirling has commercial and industrial functions. It is an important livestock market and associated with this are agricultural engineering, the manufacture of fertilizer and the production and marketing of agricultural and horticultural seeds. Stirling's largest industry is the manufacture of cigarettes, but it also produces carpets, confectionery and linoleum.

128

A new phase in the history of the town began in 1967 with the arrival of 150 undergraduates and 30 post-graduates for the new University of Stirling. The most striking features for the tourist are the reconstructed old town and the ancient castle, which looks down on the burgh from its superb vantage point on the summit of a sill of igneous rock.

# INVERARAY; Argyllshire

Inveraray is the oldest royal burgh in Argyll. In the early eighteenth century the original settlement was demolished and the 3rd Duke of Argyll, an improving laird, set about rebuilding a new town to complement his new castle, in the style of a French château. This view extends southwards over Loch Fyne and shows the castle in its rich formal setting of lands, parks and forests on a meander loop of the river Aray. The road south to Campbeltown skirts the lochside. The hill in the foreground is Duniquoich (260 m) which is surmounted by a tower.

The town stands on the flat eastern shore of Loch Fyne which was renowned for its prosperous herring fisheries and which gave the burgh its motto 'Semper tibi pendeat Halec', 'May you always have a catch of herring'. There is a weekly steamer service from Gourock to Inveraray in summer and it is a popular tourist centre. A national and civic effort resulted in the improvement of its eighteenth-century buildings: both the dwelling houses and shop fronts have an integrated scheme of decoration. Haddington in East Lothian is another town where a planned treatment of colour and design has been applied to frontages. Other Scottish burghs could benefit greatly by their example, and by the construction of new buildings in harmony with the old.

Inveraray Castle is one of the great houses of Scotland which is open to visitors. It is the seat of the Campbell family and clan, whose chief is the Duke of Argyll, known in Gaelic as 'MacCailean Mor'. The position of the lairds with extensive landed estates was strategic in former times; they had responsibilities in effecting improvements and initiating technological changes; they had rights of eviction, and the social system, with its schools, churches and other amenities depended on their benevolence. These obligations have altered and the maintenance of properties now presents serious economic problems. Both the state through its grants for buildings of architectural or historic merit, and the National Trust for Scotland, have been active in conserving such places. The stately homes with their handsome policies could be a focus for country parks, and much more could be done to make them attractive to visitors. Scots are too often indifferent to their architectural heritage, and to the pleasing qualities of landscape which owes much to the improvers and the talented architects and gardeners whom they employed to shape their parks and policies. The presence of the enlightened laird has prevented much spoilation of the countryside, and there is a growing appreciation of multi-purpose land management and planning for tourists.

# OBAN; Argyllshire

Oban is a holiday resort, steamer port and fishing harbour off the Firth of Lorne. It is an example of early nineteenth-century town development in an outstanding setting on a sweeping bay guarded by the island of Kerrera whose northern tip is seen (*left centre*). Directly opposite the ruins of Dunollie Castle, stronghold of the Lords of Lorne, stand sentinel. Northwards the waters of Loch Etive meet the Firth, amid the projecting arms of the Benderloch peninsula. The long low island is Lismore, beyond which the hills of Morvern border the seaway to Loch Linnhe.

The bay is now ringed with hotels and shops, which proliferated when the railway reached Oban in 1880. The Roman Catholic cathedral can be seen in the centre of the photograph. The place name means 'the bay', and it is a natural harbour for sailing and regattas. Oban is truly a gateway to the Hebrides—to Mull and Iona, to Coll and Tiree, to Barra and South Uist. The firm of MacBrayne, whose red funnelled steamers and brightly painted buses and lorries serve the west Highlands as part of the Scottish Transport Group, has long associations with Oban. The town is a centre for touring, with car ferries encouraging island-exploring and good roads leading north through Appin to Fort William, 80 km away, and south to Knapdale and Kintyre. Ganavan Sands north of the town has bathing beaches and a caravan and camping site.

Oban is a town built on hills—Pulpit Hill, Oban Hill and Battery Hill. From Pulpit Hill (*lower left*) a superb seascape of islands and mountains crowds the horizon. Battery Hill (*right centre*) is crowned by McCaig's Tower begun as relief work for unemployed in 1897; it is a notable landmark, resembling a Roman arena and it is floodlit in summer.

In contrast to other resort towns, there has been a refusal to debase Oban's character; there is no provision of amusement arcades or garish entertainments. People holidaying in Oban feel they are in the Highlands and on the threshold of the Hebrides, and it has Gaelic concerts and Highland Games in the tourist months.

# GRANTOWN-ON-SPEY; Morayshire

In 1776 Sir James Grant, one of the notable improving lairds, founded this settlement arranged in a regular rectilinear plan by giving 'feus' of land to prospective builders and trades-people. The town has prospered; it is situated in Strathspey at a height of nearly 210 m, and the restorative properties of the fresh hill air and pine forests were appreciated in Victorian times. So began its attraction for tourists and visitors.

It has the Georgian air of the late eighteenth century, especially in its gracious square where the buildings are almost entirely constructed of granite masonry. Slow growth rather than boom progress has given Grantown a sense of harmony in the line and proportion of its high street: the regularity of the street plan has not diminished the attractiveness of the burgh. Developmental pressures of the kind which have transformed Aviemore have been resisted. It is a mature small town, with real urban qualities.

The tourist trade is now basic to Grantown's economy. The swift flowing Spey (*left*) is famous for its salmon, and fishing stances dot the riverside. The town is a first class touring centre through which the road, north to Nairn and Forres and south to Aviemore and Perth, passes. Eastwards across the Spey, routes follow the valley to Elgin or climb the Cromdale Hills to Tomintoul and thus to Deeside.

Tourism through the year, instead of in the summer months, was ushered in with the winter sports developments in the Cairngorm Mountains, 32 km to the south. Hotels have been modernized and extended to meet new

custom, and apres-ski activities are gay and varied. Pony trekking, golf, tennis and other outdoor pursuits are popular in the summer months.

# INVERNESS; Inverness-shire

Inverness, the capital of the Highlands, is the centre of a wide and distinctive region. It stands at the river mouth of the Ness, from which it takes its name, and is the best crossing place at the northern end of Glenmore—it is a focal point for road and rail transport in northern Scotland.

In the town, traffic has to negotiate narrow streets and bridges. The town centre which lies near the river has several new buildings, one of which houses the Highlands and Islands Development Board. The riverside, with its skyline of church spires, has attractive parks and walks, with views to Inverness Castle, a handsome Victorian building fronting the Ness.

Inverness is an administrative and commercial, rather than a manufacturing town, but it has new as well as long established industries, such as distilling, tweed and knitwear production. Several government offices are located in Inverness and the professions of law, education and medicine are well represented; it has also been considered as the site for a new university.

As its significance has grown as a holiday centre, and as the advantages of living in a Highland setting are more widely appreciated, a rising population of over thirty thousand people has been drawn from surrounding districts. Rural–urban drift is a common theme in Highland Scotland where towns and villages have expanded at the expense of landward areas.

Inverness is a port: the harbour lies on the right bank of the river below the Waterloo Bridge, and handles traffic mainly with the Continent. The Kessock Ferry plies the 0·8 km channel between the Moray and Beauly Firths, to the Black Isle, which it brings within commuting distance of the town.

The people of Inverness are often praised for their well spoken English, which impressed Daniel Defoe on his tour of Scotland in 1723, when he recorded that in Inverness he found as good English as in London, perhaps because it was an acquired language in Gaelic-speaking districts. Although Gaelic is rarely heard in Inverness, the functions and character of the town are inseparably bound to Highland history and tradition.

# KIRKWALL; Orkney

Orkney has sixty-seven islands of which about twenty are inhabited. It is an island county with its own 'mainland' lying 32 km north of Caithness. On the 'mainland' stands the city of Kirkwall a town of four thousand people. The Cathedral of St. Magnus (*right centre*) is nine centuries old; apart from Glasgow, Kirkwall is the only city in Scotland to preserve structurally undamaged its pre-Reformation Cathedral, which is the proud property of the town council.

Although settlement did not begin with the Viking invaders, the town's origins are deep in the Norse past, which shows clearly in place names and Orcadian family names. This island people will not let the visitor forget that they only became part of Scotland on account of a pawning arrangement between the Scottish and Danish crowns in 1469. Orkney has been largely untouched by the upheavals of Scottish history, whether religious, economic or political.

The harbour at Kirkwall Bay faces north on the south-east side of the mainland. The Peerie Sea is across the barrier to the right. Orkney contends with relative remoteness from suppliers and markets, aggravated by increases in freight charges. The types of vessel employed on the services are considered out of date; ships capable of transporting vehicles and container traffic with quick on-and-off loading have been recommended. There are steamer connections to Aberdeen and Scrabster, as well as to Shetland and the northern isles, but the isolation of communities on the north and west periphery of Britain has had adverse economic and social consequences. A lesson might be taken from Islay where an independent company, operating a Norwegian-style vessel, has successfully broken into the transport scene.

Although Kirkwall is a trading and fishing port, with Scandinavian and Baltic ties, Orkney's economy is essentially land-based. Though virtually treeless, Orkney is a rich agricultural county which achieves not only a high degree of self sufficiency in meat, milk and dairy products from its 3,000 farms, run by progressive owner-occupiers, but is an exporter of dairy produce. The holdings average 12 to 20 ha and some would benefit by reorganization to increase their size.

Kirkwall appeals to the tourist—its streets are paved over between the shops and houses which, with their crow-stepped gables, have a continental touch. Orkney offers broad horizons of farm and field stretching to the sea to be enjoyed in the invigorating northern air.

# LERWICK; Shetland

The county of Zetland, 17 km north of Orkney consists of over 100 islands, of which fewer than twenty are inhabited. Forming the most northerly part of Britain, the isles are Norse by tradition; social, cultural and economic links have never been severed, as Shetland only came into Scottish possession in the fifteenth century as part of a marriage dowry. The nearest big town to Lerwick is Bergen in Norway, and Lerwick has stronger affinities with Scandinavia than with Scotland.

Lerwick's houses are built seawards, compactly and robustly for protection against boreal tempests, and its older streets are surfaced with flagstones. The sheltered harbour, shielded by the island of Bressay, is used by vessels from all over northern Europe, and also by its own fishing fleet geared for white fish and herring catches. Here the North of Scotland Shipping Company flagship, *St. Ninian* is at the pier.

For generations, Shetland's economy has been sea based. Hence the people are seafarers first and only part-time crofters, whereas Orcadians are farmers with boats. Shetlanders experience not only the hardships of isolation, and soaring transport costs, but also the erosion of independent local management of such services as police and water supplies. There are steamer and air services to Orkney and Shetland. Heavy freight charges are forcing Shetlanders to look to Scandinavia for supplies and invidious comparisons are drawn with the Faeroes where population is being held and wealth is increasing.

Kindly folk and alluring scenery have made Shetland a tourist's delight. People devise their own entertainments, enjoying fiddle music; the mid-winter festival 'Up-Helly-Aa' which celebrates the return of the sun is an opportunity to go Viking. In summer, there is sailing and fishing in the voes, or sea inlets.

Shetland's small breeds of pony, sheep and dog are unique. Shetland sheep are plucked or 'rooed'; their wool

is exceptionally soft and warm. Knitwear and fine cloths,
are produced by cottage-based or small factory industries
whose exports exceed £1·5 million each year. Shetland is in
the forefront of oil exploration.

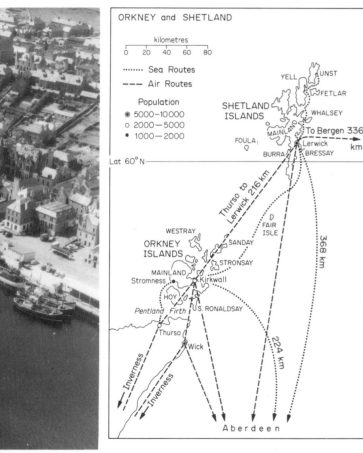

ORKNEY and SHETLAND

kilometres

0   20   40   60   80

········ Sea Routes

--- Air Routes

Population
⊙ 5000–10000
○ 2000–5000
• 1000–2000

SHETLAND
ISLANDS

YELL    UNST
        FETLAR
        WHALSEY

FOULA

MAINLAND

BURRA    BRESSAY

Lerwick    To Bergen 336
                        km

Lat 60° N

Thurso to Lerwick 216 km

368 km

WESTRAY

ORKNEY
ISLANDS

SANDAY

STRONSAY

FAIR
ISLE

MAINLAND
Stromness    Kirkwall

HOY

S. RONALDSAY

Pentland Firth

Thurso

Wick

224 km

Inverness

Inverness

A b e r d e e n

Right: wild scenery on Unst

# GLENEAGLES; Perthshire

Man's interference over the centuries has transformed the Scottish landscape from coast to mountain top to greater or lesser extent. Changing heath or forest into farmland has been one endeavour of reclamation; this view shows another type.

Gleneagles is a celebrated golfing mecca, with a palatial railway hotel, open in summer, which cossets the affluent with every luxury. It boasts five stars, with all that this implies in excellence, but it is its golf courses, two of eighteen holes known as the King's and the Queen's and one nine-hole course, which are the undoubted attraction. These courses have been sculpted out of hummocky moors lying between Strathearn and Strathallan. The knolls and ridges are fluvio-glacial deposits spread initially by meltwater flowing eastwards from the Highland ice cap. The Lowland is thus overlaid by a moundy surface of sands and gravels, termed 'kames' (knolls), 'kettles' (hollows) and 'eskers' (ridges). Sand and gravel pits to supply the construction industry have devastated such landforms in Lowland Scotland. Small channel-like features forming interconnected systems, which mark the passage of glacial waters, are also common on stretches of the Highland border, which lies just north of Gleneagles.

Here is terrain eminently suitable for smoothing and dressing into greens and fairways, for excavating into bunkers and for peppering with trees and bushes to trap those who cannot hit the ball straight. Challenging to the player, but pleasing to the eye, the Gleneagles courses are among the most beautiful in Britain.

Around Gleneagles are the broad fields of Strathallan, drained and improved by long cultivation. Bitter winds sweep along the Strath in winter—hence the trees are not only decorative but protective. Tracts of moorland still remain and afford rough shooting. The main railway and road (*right*) from Stirling to Perth streak across Strathearn towards the village of Auchterarder.

# MUIRFIELD; East Lothian

Muirfield is one of three golf courses situated close to Gullane in East Lothian where a sand dune strip on raised beach deposits has been adapted for the purpose. Scotland's place in golf is unique as it is the home of the game, whose traditional and active seat of government is the Royal and Ancient Club in St. Andrews, Fife—its rules extend to the ends of the earth. Scotland has a reputation for testing courses like the Old Course at St. Andrews, Old Troon and Turnberry on the Ayrshire coast and Carnoustie.

Muirfield's fame is also worldwide; it was begun in 1891 and is owned by the Honourable Company of Edinburgh Golfers. Measuring 6,280 m in length, it was the setting for the Open Championship in 1972. This view shows the Open in progress. The course is thronged with spectators, clustering round the greens and tees as they follow their fancy.

A full length golf course consists of eighteen holes—the tees, the fairways and the greens, which should be as smooth as a billiard table. Bordering the fairway is the rough—commonly unshorn grass, whins and bushes or trees, where a misplaced shot results in a soaring score—and there are appropriate clubs for every emergency. Golf is scored in the number of strokes taken from each tee until the putt on the green is sunk. Breaking seventy-five at Muirfield would be a cause for congratulations.

Gentle but thorough exercise is assured because the player will walk 6·4 km to go round this course. Muirfield is for 'men only' but the advantage of golf is that it may be played at all seasons, by both men and women, and by people of all ages. It may be enjoyed by the solitary, but competitive and friendly company is preferable. The game has growing popularity—there are about 250,000 active and dilettante golfers in Scotland and there are some 400 golf courses.

Since 1945 about fifteen new courses have been developed; surprisingly few have been lost to the game. More could be constructed with advantage—a full sized course requires 48 ha of land, with the cost depending on the nature of the terrain. Adding equipment and a club house £30,000 might be the sum, although a nine hole or pitch and putt course could be had for a more modest expenditure. Such an investment would provide years of pleasurable recreation, but 'golf club' has become confused with 'country club' which gives intending players the impression that it is an expensive and exclusive sport. The majority of Scotland's golf enthusiasts would correct this opinion.

# THE AVIEMORE CENTRE, Inverness-shire

Aviemore is the nearest Speyside village to the ski slopes of the Cairngorms, and has multiplied in size and complexity with the development of the Aviemore Centre.

A hundred years ago Aviemore consisted of an inn and two farms on the road to Inverness, but the village began to grow with the opening of the railway; summer visitors came in increasing numbers to explore the mountain landscapes rich in forest and lochs. In spite of its Victorian hotels and villas, Aviemore's focus was its rail junction and station (*foreground*), and the village itself was straggling and undistinguished.

The proximity of Aviemore to the Cairngorms, its position on the A9 trunk road and on the main line to Inverness from the south have been outstanding locational advantages. There has been a skiing boom, fostered by the affluence of young people. The first major hotel project was the siting of a motor inn near Coylumbridge; thereafter the Aviemore Centre was constructed on ground formerly occupied by a station hotel and golf course. It is a joint enterprise by brewing and retail companies—accommodation varies from luxury hotel suites to inexpensive chalets, and at all seasons a very wide range of sports and leisure facilities is provided.

The Aviemore Centre has a magnificent setting of crags and birchwood; the towering heights of Craigellachie from which the Clan Grant takes its rallying 'Standfast Craigellachie', rises at its back, and is an outlier of the Monadhliath. The buildings are (*left to right*), the Strathspey Hotel, visible from every vantage point, the Osprey Room with its halls and restaurants, the Badenoch Hotel, the curling and skating rink and the swimming pool are grouped round a paved courtyard (*centre*). The Aviemore chalets are to the right. There are also shops, car parks and an artificial ski slope (*right centre*). The Aviemore Centre has much to commend it although it is raw and still shows the scars of construction. An official report estimated that by 1967 the employment level would be increased by 1,000 jobs but not all positions can be filled locally.

The lack of preparation of the countryside for the hordes of car-tourists coming to Aviemore is evident.

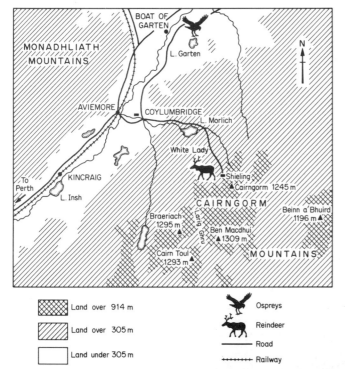

Land over 914 m
Land over 305 m
Land under 305 m
Ospreys
Reindeer
Road
Railway

Roadsides, fields and pine forests are scattered with litter and devastated by fire. If there are no measures to control touristic abuses Scotland may become 'the worst tourist slum in Europe'. The Countryside Commission and all concerned with tourism have a vital role to play here; the county councils are responsible for roadside cleansing and the Litter Act requires enforcement. To spread tourist pressures, more caravan and camping sites are wanted—with a ban on picnic fires outside specified areas. A country warden or forest ranger service, which would combine de-termination to stop abuses, with helpfulness and guidance, is a necessity.

The Aviemore region shows too plainly the folly of letting loose multitudes on a countryside almost totally unprepared to receive them. Similar projects to that of the centre must ensure that substantial investment is ex-pended on adequate tourist facilities and services in the surrounding district, not as an afterthought but as part of the infrastructure of development.

# GLEN SHEE; Perthshire

Glen Shee is one of the three leading ski grounds of Scotland. The shapely massif of the Cairnwell (933 m) stands guard above the Perth-Braemar road. From Spittal of Glenshee (*upper centre*) the route winds up Glen Beag, leading to the ski slopes on Meall Odhar, Glas Maol and the Cairnwell. The abrupt bend in the road (*left centre*) is the famous Devil's Elbow whose steep hair-pin bends have been much improved in recent years. It is still noted as one of the first routes in Scotland to be blocked by snow in winter, and it is protected by long snow fences to arrest drifting. It is also a popular summer touring route to Braemar and Royal Deeside.

A chairlift station, a restaurant, car parks and ski-tows have been constructed (*lower right*). Sudden changes in the weather, and in particular strong winds, which prevent the operation of chairlifts, denude slopes of snow cover and block access roads with snow, are probably the biggest handicaps to the development of Scottish skiing. This is not surprising for the climate of Scottish mountains is Arctic rather than Alpine in character. April to May is probably the best season, with crisp spring snow glittering in the corries, and luring the novice and the expert to the hills.

Apart from winter and spring holiday weekends, summer brings brisker business to the chairlifts, when tourists are eager to sample rapid-transit to the high tops to enjoy the incomparable vistas which are normally only attainable by the able and determined walker. Visitors going mountain exploring are advised to take water- and windproof clothing, a sufficiency of food, and to have regard to warnings displayed at the chairlift stations.

There is a double chairlift system in Coire Cas in the Cairngorms; the White Corries Chairlift operates on Meall a'Bhuiridh (1,109 m) in Glencoe: the city of Edinburgh has a chairlift and artificial ski slope in the Pentland hills to provide training and practice, as well as a fine viewpoint for non-skiers.

# THE CUILLINS; Isle of Skye

Scotland's highest mountains are small compared with continental peaks like the Alps, or the Fjell of Norway, but they should not be underestimated. Perhaps it is the ruggedness and infinite variety of the Scottish mountains which have made rock climbing and hill walking the enthusiasms of so many Scots. There are 543 summits over (914 m) in height which come into the category of 'Munroes'.

For mountaineers, the Cuillins in Skye with their tough gabbro offer some of the finest pitches in the world ranging from the easy to the most severe, and fifteen of the tops are over 914 m high.

The Isle of Skye is a winged island of sea lochs and peninsulas with sharply contrasted landscapes. It is composed essentially of tertiary igneous rocks, which geologists find rewarding. The Cuillins are not mountains for solitary expeditions by the unprepared and foolhardy. Sudden weather changes with sea mists and gales demand watchfulness. Even the rough walking over low ground requires wind- and waterproof clothing and strong footwear.

In the photograph the Black Cuillins with their serrated edges stand impregnable beyond the more rounded granitic Red Cuillin. The coast road skirting Broadford Bay leads north west towards Sligachan and Portree. In the foreground the crofts of Breakish, Skulamus and Harripool follow the roadside like beads on a string. Eastwards the road continues to Kyleakin, which is linked to the mainland by ferry at Kyle of Lochalsh. There is a proposal to build a £3 million bridge at the narrows; meantime new ferries have been introduced to relieve summer congestion. There is no Sunday service out of deference to local opinion, which some would interpret as a brake on tourism, and others as a feature of Skye which is to be welcomed in a restless society. A car ferry service operates from Uig in the north-west of Skye to the Outer Hebrides and tourist expansion is planned for the port.

# KIPPFORD; Kirkcudbright

The increasing popularity of small boat sailing is all part of Britain's leisure boom. City dwellers who sail at weekends on gravel pits and reservoirs travel to loch and inlet for their summer holidays. For such people the appeal of the sheltered bays of Britain's western coasts is strong. Kippford on the Solway Firth has all the characteristic attractions of the coastline of Wigtownshire and Kirkcudbright for the sailor: the inlet is a sheltered ria with a hinterland of hill, moor and woodland, yet it is accessible from the A74 and the trans-Pennine routes for visitors from the south. Caravan and camping sites provide basic facilities for the tourist and there are some fine golf courses near by.

Sailing is a recreation in which the participant brings his own equipment and asks for little more of his holiday base than a water surface and sufficient wind to fill his sails. In very popular places there are demands for yachting marinas, which are rare in Scotland. They will certainly increase in the future, but it is just as certain that there will always be many sailors who seek nothing more than a quiet bay in unspoilt country, such as this stretch of south-west Scotland offers.

# NAIRN; County of Nairn

Situated on the southern shore of the Moray Firth, Nairn is a small burgh which provides holiday facilities similar to those found in many towns and villages along Scotland's east coast. Safe bathing on sandy beaches, challenging golf courses, a variety of tours by mountain and loch in the immediate hinterland, and the absence of large-scale urban and commercial developments, from which many holidaymakers seek to escape, lure visitors to these towns.

The post-war tourist boom, associated with longer paid holidays and increased car ownership, has resulted in a demand for accommodation which many resorts have been unable to supply. Camping and caravanning have offered partial solutions to the problem. The popularity of caravanning has put pressure on amenity values. While a few isolated caravans may be tolerated on a stretch of coast or lochside, whole static caravan villages are unsightly and may, if uncontrolled, destroy the very features which first attracted visitors to the area.

That there is a demand for caravan sites is obvious to anyone who has tried to drive hastily along highland roads in the summer months. So heavy is the touring caravan traffic on roads unsuited to their size, that some narrower roads are being closed to caravanners.

There is also a great need for well-prepared sites. In 1969 a Civic Trust Award was made to the Yellowcraigs Caravan Site in East Lothian, where the parking space had been arranged more attractively than usual and the site was well screened. Here at Nairn the local authority has provided a limited site with easy access to the beach and the golf course. Only by this careful planning can amenity values be preserved and good facilities for the holiday-maker be provided.

# JOHN O'GROATS; Caithness

Scotland's Land's End is named after a Dutchman, and not a Scotsman as might have been expected. It is not the most northerly point on the mainland either; this distinction rests with Dunnet Head, a promontory some 18 km to the west of John O'Groats. John de Groot, a Dutchman, lived in the vicinity in the fifteenth century. It is claimed that he ran the Orkney ferry linking the mainland with the islands.

In good weather, the eagerness with which travellers approach John O'Groats is rewarded by fine views of sea cliffs. To the north west is Stroma Island, further north across the Pentland Firth, the boisterous seaway between the Atlantic and the North Sea, can be seen Hoy and South Ronaldsay, the southernmost islands of Orkney.

Despite an erroneous claim to fame, John O'Groats is linked in the popular imagination with Land's End, the western tip of Cornwall located 1,406 km away. Between these points are routes used by car rally enthusiasts, coach tours, marathon walkers and racing cyclists. A small cottage tea room is the solitary welcome afforded to these long-distance travellers at John O'Groats.

# Nursing and Working with Other People

## Series Editor: Shirley Bach

**Transforming Nursing Practice – titles in the series**

| | |
|---|---|
| Law and Professional Issues in Nursing | ISBN 978 1 84445 160 9 |
| Nursing and Working with Other People | ISBN 978 1 84445 161 6 |
| Nursing in Contemporary Healthcare Practice | ISBN 978 1 84445 159 3 |

To order, contact our distributor: BEBC Distribution, Albion Close, Parkstone, Poole, BH12 3LL. Telephone: 0845 230 9000, email: **learningmatters@bebc.co.uk**. You can also find more information on each of these titles and our other learning resources at **www.learningmatters.co.uk**